Report on Regulatory Agencies
to the President-Elect

ԳP

REPORT ON REGULATORY AGENCIES TO THE PRESIDENT-ELECT

*Submitted by the Chairman of the Subcommittee on
Administrative Practice and Procedure to the
Committee on the Judiciary of the United States Senate*

BY

JAMES M. LANDIS

ꟼP

QUID PRO BOOKS
New Orleans, Louisiana

REPORT ON REGULATORY AGENCIES TO THE PRESIDENT-ELECT

Part of the *Legal Legends Series* from Quid Pro Books.

ISBN 978-1-61027-249-0 (pbk)
ISBN 978-1-61027-248-3 (ebk)

QUID PRO BOOKS

5860 Citrus Blvd.

Suite D-101

New Orleans, Louisiana 70123

www.quidprobooks.com

qp

REPORT ON REGULATORY AGENCIES TO THE PRESIDENT-ELECT

James M. Landis
December 1960

December 21, 1960

My dear Senator:

I am submitting herewith my report on the regulatory agencies. I regret its length but the subject is a broad one. In the section entitled "Summary and Conclusions" I have set forth as recommendations the major suggestions contained in the report. They will in my opinion greatly improve the operation of these agencies and also carry out suggestions that you have previously made as well as the pledges contained in the program of your party.

I have emphasized the coordination of policy, now sadly lacking, in the fields of transportation, communications and energy. If we must — and you have rightly said we must — step up the pace of our economic growth in order to assure both our primacy and our survival in this dangerous world, the acceleration of that pace depends upon our ability to develop and implement effective national policies within these fields.

I have also dwelt quite heavily in a section entitled "Personnel" on the matter of the qualifications that should be required of the men called upon to man these agencies. No better service could be rendered to the administrative agencies as a whole than by gradually restaffing them with men who, because of their competence and their desire to fulfill the legislative mandates described in the basic statutes establishing these agencies, will inspire a sense of devotion to and pride in the public service by their many employees.

I am indebted to many individuals for the contribution of data and ideas upon which this report is based. It is impossible to mention all of them, particularly the many individuals in the agencies with whom I have had a long-time association and whose intimate knowledge of the operations of these agencies has been invaluable. Also, I am indebted to numerous practitioners before these agencies who have manifested a desire to promote their efficiency rather than some individual interest. I should like particularly to express my appreciation for the cooperation given me by the Congress, the various agencies, and the Executive Branch of the Government particularly the Bureau of the Budget and to the members and the staff of the Committees of the Senate and the House of Representatives headed by Senator Carroll and Congressman Harris. I should also like to express my gratitude to my associates who have given most generously of their time to this work.

In conclusion, I want to express my thanks to you for this opportunity to reevaluate a governmental process that has been a continuing concern of mine for some thirty years.

Sincerely yours,

James M. Landis

Senator John F. Kennedy
United States Senate
Washington, D. C.

TABLE OF CONTENTS

INTRODUCTION [1]

I. THE PROBLEMS [4]

    A. Delays in the Disposition of Adjudicatory Proceedings [6]

    B. Costs [8]

    C. Personnel [12]

    D. Ethical Conduct [14]

    E. Administrative Procedures [16]

    F. Administrative Organization [19]

    G. The Formulation of Policy Within the Agency [24]

    H. Inter-Agency Policy Formulation [27]

    I. Relationship of the Agencies to the Executive [33]

    J. Relationship of the Agencies to the Legislative [37]

II. SUGGESTED REMEDIES [39]

    A. Delay, Costs and Agency Organization [40]

        1. The Interstate Commerce Commission [41]

        2. The Civil Aeronautics Board [46]

3. The Securities and Exchange Commission [50]

4. The Federal Trade Commission [54]

5. The Federal Communications Commission [59]

6. The Federal Power Commission [62]

7. The National Labor Relations Board [66]

8. Other Regulatory Agencies [74]

9. Action Immediately Desirable [74]

B. Personnel [75]

C. Ethical Conduct and Industry Orientation [78]

D. Administrative Procedure [82]

E. The Coordination of Agency Policy [84]

F. Relationship of the Agencies to the Executive and the Legislative [92]

SUMMARY AND CONCLUSIONS [94]

About the Author [101]

Note to the 2014 Reprint Edition: Page numbers above and at bottom of text pages, though roughly corresponding to the original pagination, specifically follow the modern formatting and presentation of this edition.

REPORT ON REGULATORY AGENCIES TO THE PRESIDENT-ELECT

INTRODUCTION

The general problem of the administrative agencies and their role in government has been a subject of consideration for the past twenty-five years by various branches of the government, bar associations and legal and political science scholars. These studies, extremely voluminous in character, have ranged over many topics from the fairness of the procedures employed in the adjudication of cases to the relationship that these agencies should bear to the Executive on the one hand and to the Legislative Branch of the Government on the other. Specific proposals for the internal reorganization or consolidation of various agencies have emanated from time to time and to a degree have become effective through legislation or through such powers as they have been delegated to the President under the various Reorganization Acts.

There has been no lack of concern with the general problem but, viewing the subject in the large, the concrete results achieved by these voluminous studies bear a very small ratio to the time and effort that the studies and investigations themselves have consumed.

Effective procedural solutions, so necessary to the proper functioning of the administrative agencies, have admittedly not been achieved despite the sweeping studies which culminated in the Administrative Procedure Act of 1946 and the many studies which have followed. Spectacular instances of executive, legislative and industry interference with the disposition of matters before the agencies have been uncovered. Expansion of the role, power and duties of the agencies has continued and despite the absence of effective solution of and increasing concern with their problems they now embrace within their regulatory powers almost every significant aspect of our national being.

Their continued existence is obviously essential for effective government. The complexities of our modern society are increasing rather than decreasing. The advent of atomic energy, of telecommunications, of natural gas, of jet aircraft, to cite only a few examples, all call for greater surveillance by government of the appropriate use of these resources to further the admittedly dim but recognizable aims of our society.

A reappraisal of the various functions and activities of the regulatory agencies is thus desirable at this very critical period of our national life for reasons that are only too apparent. The scope of responsibility entrusted to these agencies is enormous, exceeding in its sweep, from the standpoint of its economic impact perhaps, the powers remaining in the Executive and the Legislative. This is true despite the fact that such powers as they exercise are generally delegated to them by the Legislative. This delegation followed upon the conviction that the problems in a particular area were so manifold and complex that the Congress simply had neither the time nor the capacity to handle them. Similarly the delegation to them of adjudicatory powers stemmed from the conviction that the issues involved were different from those that theretofore had been traditionally handled by courts and thus were not suited for judicial determination. These delegations, once made, are rarely recalled or retracted; on the contrary, the tendency is to expand them as more and more complex problems arise. The legislative standards under which the delegations are made are similarly increasingly loosened so that not infrequently the guide in the determination of problems that face the agencies is not much more than their conception of the public interest.

This reappraisal to be of any value as a guide for action must have concreteness. Mere generalities will be useless. Nevertheless, absent generalizations that can be spelled out of facts, forward and constructive thinking is difficult. The experience of the past twenty-five years cannot be overlooked, nor can the existence of a problem in one agency be evaluated without the recognition that it has basic common aspects with like problems in other agencies. The approach, moreover, must be impartial in the sense that it should neither be a diatribe against the administrative process — a tendency characteristic of able but older scholars of the 1930's; nor should it have a bias in favor of the administrative disposition of matters, an attitude not uncommon among government servants too imbued with the bureaucracies that they administer.

Finally, it must be remembered that we cannot regard our government as simply a government of laws and not of men, but rather a government of laws by men. Although the mechanisms we create for administration may be more or less well adapted to a particular task, the individuals that operate them singly or as a group have the ultimate responsibility of guidance and control.

The results of their operations will thus reflect not only efficiency or inefficiency but more importantly the ideals and goals that within the framework of the basic law can fairly be achieved.

I. THE PROBLEMS

There is no single solution which can be projected for problems common to all the regulatory agencies. Indeed, no one can even correctly define the term "regulatory agency," or enumerate the group that comes within such a concept. Classification of these agencies under the category of "independent" or "executive" is also meaningless. No rational line has been pursued by the Congress in differentiating the "independent" agencies from those embraced within some Executive Department. The regulation of stock exchanges, for example, has been delegated to an "independent" agency whereas the regulation of commodity exchanges is under the jurisdiction of an Executive Department. Similarly misrepresentation in the sale of articles, including drugs, is the concern of an independent agency, whereas so-called mislabeling of foods, drugs and insecticides, which reaches far beyond the mere label, is a concern of an Executive Department.

At various times in the last twenty-five years so-called general problems came to the surface. Twenty or more years ago the procedural aspect of administrative regulation and adjudication was the uppermost problem. The prime emphasis then was placed on the combination of prosecuting and adjudicatory functions within the same agency. It was the concern with this problem that led eventually to the passage of the Administrative Procedure Act of 1946 with its emphasis upon the internal separation of these functions within the agency and the granting of some degree of independence to the hearing examiners. It was the same emphasis that altered the pattern in 1947 of the National Labor Relations Board to deprive the Board of much of its power to initiate proceedings, transferring this function to an independent General Counsel — an experiment which after a decade of trial and error is not likely to be repeated.

Of late the emphasis has shifted to questions of conflicts of interest and ex parte presentations as well as to an effort to transfer certain adjudicatory functions to administrative tribunals or courts. The tendency here is again further to judicialize the administrative process and, in the opinion of many observers, to over-judicialize it to a point where stagnation is likely to set in. More recently a less legalistic approach has been taken, namely to treat the agency as more of a managerial mechanism so as to free it in its broader aspects from the burdens entailed by judicial requirements. This, for example, is the basic thought underlying such studies as those of Professor Emmette S. Redford of the University of Texas and those initiated through various management consultant firms by the Bureau of the Budget.

All of these have had then value and in then way have alleviated certain distressing tendencies becoming apparent on the administrative scene. Certain fundamental problems have, however, not been solved. On the contrary, their persistence is too serious to be longer ignored, for their prevalence is threatening to thwart hopes so bravely held some two decades ago by those who believed that the administrative agency, particularly the "independent" agency, held within it the seeds for the wise and efficient solution of the many new problems posed by a growingly complex society and a growingly benevolent government. It is to these problems that this report addresses itself.

A. Delays in the Disposition of Adjudicatory Proceedings

Inordinate delay characterizes the disposition of adjudicatory proceedings before substantially all of our regulatory agencies. In the Civil Aeronautics Board, for example, the average age of dockets closed by formal proceedings in 1960 was some 32 months. As of June 30, 1959, out of 464 proceedings then pending, 166 had been pending for more than 3 years. The Federal Trade Commission as of June 30, 1959, had 309 cease and desist orders pending, of which 118 had been pending for more than one year and 30 for more than 3 years. In the Federal Power Commission the backlog of pending cases in 1959 was almost four times as great as in 1957. Only last September that Commission announced that it would take 13 years with its present staff to clear up its pending 2,313 producer rate cases pending as of July 1, 1960, and that with the contemplated 6500 cases that would be filed during that 13 year period it could not become current until 2043 A.D. even if its staff were tripled. Contested proceedings before the Interstate Commerce Commission tend to run from 18 to 36 months, and numerous proceedings before the Federal Communications Commission and the Maritime Board have been pending for more than 3 years. The statutory period of 20 days during which a normal registration statement covering the issuance of new securities becomes effective under the Securities Act of 1933 has in practice been lengthened to some 40 to 60 days. Numerous similar statistics can be gathered from other agencies, including individual instances when even 10 and 14 years have elapsed before a final determination has been made. They all corroborate the fact of interminable delay.

The causes making for delay are not uniform. Some are due to inadequate budgets. A period of economic rigor, if not parsimony seems to have characterized the Bureau of the Budget's attitude toward the various agencies beginning in 1952, an attitude that was slowly being relaxed in 1960. During the fiscal year 1950, when 496 registration statements were filed with the Securities and Exchange Commission, the Bureau of the Budget approved 1,130 employees for the Commission, of which 1060 were authorized by Congress. As of fiscal year 1955 with 849 registration statements filed with the Commission only 717 employees were approved by the Budget Bureau of which 699 were authorized by Congress. As of fiscal year 1960 with 1628 registration statements filed with the Commission only 978 employees had been approved by the Budget Bureau of which 954 were authorized by Congress Obviously either extravagance characterized the situation in 1950 or parsimony in 1960. In any event, the statutory waiting period during that decade was in substance tripled. Similar situations prevailed in many other agencies.

The blame, if any, for this situation does not rest purely on the Budget Bureau. The agency heads themselves, presumably under the general direction of the Executive Office of the President, curtailed their requests despite the growing pressure of the business pending before them for disposition. Congress similarly exhibited the same tendencies. Indeed, despite the decision of the Supreme Court of the United States in the *Phillips* case in 1954 (347 U. S. 672) empowering in the Federal Power Commission to fix rates for producers of natural gas and clearly envisaging a need for greatly expanded personnel, a request for a supplemental appropriation of $300,000 was cut to $100,000.

Some causes for delay are peculiar to the particular agency. Following the *Phillips* case, the Federal Power Commission was flooded with rate filings by the numerous producers of natural gas. In general, these new rates were allowed to go into effect on the condition that any reductions later determined by the Commission should be refunded to the consumers. Since legislation was shortly thereafter introduced to deprive the Commission of this aspect of its rate-making power, the Commission appears to have refrained from any real effort to deal with its docket on the theory that the passage of these bills, in the manner of a *deus ex machina*, would relieve them totally and finally of this sudden accretion in their business. The bills, however, were vetoed on two occasions and the problem in an immensely exaggerated form still rests on the door step of the Commission, since rate increase has now been pancaked upon rate increase. The consequences of this inaction have been serious, particularly to the individual natural gas consumers since, unlike the large industrial consumers, they cannot easily convert to a cheaper fuel and thus benefit from the restraint placed upon rising prices to industrial consumers by the existence of competitive fuel prices.

The situation in the Federal Communications Commission appears to derive from other causes, primarily the inability of that Commission to make up its mind on some of the broad issues that face it. Despite the patent failure evident by 1955 of the allocation system devised in 1952 to provide a viable economic life for users of the UHF frequencies in the same market, five years have now elapsed without any appreciable dent being made on this problem. True, during these years an extensive investigation was made by other sources of this problem, primarily by the Subcommittee on Communications of the Senate Committee on Interstate and Foreign Commerce. The Communications Commission, like the Federal Power Commission, may have hoped that some magic formula would spring from these investigations which would relieve it of the necessity for independent courageous action. If so, that hope was stillborn and the Commission's problem still remains. Here again delay has serious consequences on the destiny of television, for additional VHF channels have not been made available with the result that the existing monopoly of the established networks, particularly in the two TV channel markets, cannot economically be challenged by existing or potential programming entities. The recent action of the Commission in instituting a rule-making proceeding which may make available some VHF frequencies in one and two station markets may be something of a palliative to this situation but it is hardly a comprehensive answer.

The chief causes of these many delays, however, are the growing business before the regulatory agencies. Mere budget increases only occasionally will give an answer to this congestion. If these cases require disposition by the agency heads themselves, increases in the subordinate staff are not the answer. Far more searching answers are required, some of which are discussed at a later stage in this report. This is not to say that the agencies will not have before them over the years to come cases of complexity that will take years to conclude. But even with respect to these cases, measures to make less rather than more complex what is an inherently complex problem, must be devised.

B. Costs

Originally it was believed that a public benefit would ensue from the fact that the cost of pursuing an administrative remedy would be substantially less than the existing method of resort to the courts. This hope has not been realized except in those instances when the government itself has the duty in the public interest to pursue a remedy which otherwise would have had to be pursued by the private individual.

Studies as to the extent of these costs — strange as it may seem — have not been made. Apart from the costs to the individual petitioner, the costs to the government itself must be considered. The overall costs themselves derive from two factors: first, the time element involved in waiting for an ultimate administrative determination and judicial review, if any, and, second, the length of the hearings that precede such a determination. Given a hearing with a record of some 20,000 pages, the costs merely of the acquisition of that record alone will total some $20,000. Additional costs in the preparation of numerous exhibits, the hiring of experts, such as engineers and accountants, fees paid to lawyers, and the expenses of housing and feeding this group of men during the weeks of hearings, bring the total to a very substantial sum. If some twenty or thirty participants or intervenors are involved in the proceeding, the overall cost becomes staggering. In the *Seven States Case* before the Civil Aeronautics Board, in which there were 150 parties and intervenors with 225 appearances noted and in which hearings lasted for 20 days, or the *Phillips Petroleum Co.* rate case before the Federal Power Commission in which 76 lawyers entered appearances for 33 parties and intervenors and in which the hearings consumed 82 days and oral argument before the Commission two further days, the total costs must have run into the millions. This latter case incidentally was only a later phase of proceedings initiated in 1948, and the decision recently made in 1960 is likely to be subjected to further review.

These examples of the scope of costs are not unusual. They mean that to be successful in a petition for an important certificate of public necessity and convenience or a television or radio license the petitioner must be well-supplied with funds, which the petitioner must be willing to wager on his chances of being successful. The result is that in many situations the small businessman is practically excluded from an opportunity to compete. A factor that tends to increase these costs is that in many cases they are passed on to the public in the form of rate increases or subsidies based upon their allowance as an operating expense, so that the companies lack any real incentive to cut them down.

A further element of costs in many situations is the resort to public relations techniques to create a national atmosphere congenial to the position of a particular petitioner or intervenor — an expensive operation — in the hope that such an atmosphere will produce a decision favorable to the applicant. On several occasions the larger airlines have resorted to this technique, as well as applicants for licenses or special privileges before the Federal Communications Commission. See e.g. *American President Lines*, 7 C. A. B. 799, 818; Proceedings subsequent to the decision in *United Airlines v. C. A. B*, 278 F. (2d) 446.

Indirect costs stemming from the factor of delay in the final determination can also assume large proportions. They are difficult to measure but from testimony recently adduced they can run into the millions with respect to a particular case. Delays in the issuance of pipe-line certificates by the Federal Power Commission have resulted in increased costs of from two to ten million dollars, costs that are inevitably passed on to the public. Delays in the establishment of rates for the transportation of gas are presently holding up programs for expansion which can involve over $100 million of steel construction which in the light of the present employment of our steel capacity means much to the steel industry and the unemployment situation. Some $500 million is now held up under the suspension policy of the Federal Power Commission with reference to rates filed by natural gas producers, some of which is theoretically distributable to consumers but which practicably after the lapse of four to six years may never reach them. The delay in route cases before the Civil Aeronautics Board, such as the *Southern Transcontinental Route Case*, has held up procurement policies for commercial aircraft to an unknown degree. Delays in the time in which registration statements have become effective due to the burden of work before the Securities Exchange Commission have increased underwriting costs and forced resort to means of financing less desirable and more expensive.

C. Personnel

It is generally admitted by most observers that since World War II a deterioration in the quality of our administrative personnel has taken place, both at the top level and through-out the staff.

The causes for this are complex. The years since 1946, despite the Korean War, have been years of relative complacency as contrasted with the period from 1933 to 1941. The fires that then fed a passion for public service have burned low, making recruitment an increasingly difficult task. Careful scrutiny of agency members from the standpoint of their qualifications as well as their prejudices in behalf of administering the legisla-tive goals to which they were to be committed, was during these years too often replaced by a consideration of what political obligations could be repaid through appointments. The area of so-called Schedule C appointments, free from Civil Service requirements, was increased affecting seriously the morale of those persons who looked upon government service as a career. Advancements to choice positions were also less rarely made from the staff. Instead outsiders not infrequently less qualified were appointed to these positions.

These attitudes have had a serious impact upon the regulatory agencies. At the top level initial expertise would be lacking and the want of devotion to the public service militated against its acquisition through continuing tenure. Top administrative positions appear to have been sought frequently as stepping stones to further political preference or to positions of importance within the industries subject to regulation. A too common complaint at the bar is that the staffs have captured the commissions and that independent and bold thinking on the part of the members of these agencies is absent. These factors in turn reacted upon the staffs. Lacking challenges for creative effort, recruitment of outstanding younger men lagged perceptibly. Where in the 1930's a majority of the leading graduates of our better law schools chose public service, in the 1950's only a handful could be drawn away from the opportunities offered them by private practice. Even the spirit once displayed by the veterans of the early years ebbed through the absence of leadership at the top.

Two measures designed to cure this situation have failed to do so. The first was a general and, indeed, generous increase in compensation payable, particularly at the top and bottom rungs. But even where salaries were made comparable in large measure to those paid by private industry this situation has not been corrected. The spark, the desire for public service, has failed of re-ignition.

A second measure, designed to afford a greater opportunity for leadership to the chairmen of our important Commissions has strangely missed fire. Prior to World War II, these chairmen were generally elected by the Commission members. Often the chairmanship was rotated year by year and, as in the case of the Federal Trade Commission and the Interstate Commerce Commission, the chairman became little more than the presiding officer at commission meetings. In other commissions the chairman took a position of leadership primarily through his personality, although possessing few powers other than those possessed by his colleagues. Since World War II, reorganization plans have allowed the President to appoint the chairman and have made the chairman responsible for the administrative direction and organization of his agency. The Interstate Commerce Commission, however, succeeded in arousing sufficient Congressional pressure to defeat the application of such a plan to it.

The obvious design of this provision of the various reorganization plans was to make the chairman the contact for agency affairs with the office of the President and, by enhancing his powers, to increase his prestige and to put him in a real position of leadership with reference to his agency. The measure has failed to achieve this purpose Some chairmen, for fear of upsetting their colleagues, have not exercised the power delegated to them but referred responsibilities entrusted to them to the collective judgment of their colleagues. Some chairmen designated by the President have simply not had the qualifications or commanded the respect required to assume their rightful position. A device, that could have been of great value, has thus not been properly utilized.

D. Ethical Conduct

Much attention has recently been centered on efforts, unfortunately too frequently successful, to sway the judgment of the members of regulatory agencies by so-called *ex parte* approaches or arguments, usually personalized, made off the record in proceedings that should be decided on the record. The extent of these *ex parte* approaches has only partially been revealed. They come from various sources — the office of the President, members of the Congress, and the regulated industries. Some are made in good faith; others to further a personal desire regardless of the public interest. Many of them emanate from lawyers striving to press their clients' cause, indeed, one of the worst phases of this situation is the existence of groups of lawyers, concentrated in Washington itself, who implicitly hold out to clients that they have means of access to various regulatory agencies off the record that are more important than those that can be made on the record. These lawyers have generally previously held positions of more or less importance in the Government. The examination of the appointment diary of one of the present Commissioners gives strong inferential although not definitive proof of what these off-the-record approaches can imply.

One of the most extraordinary situations where these influences play a significant part — a situation technically legalized by the Civil Aeronautics Act — revolves about the White House itself. Under that Act the President has the ultimate determination as to which carriers shall fly what international and overseas routes. The grant of that privilege to the President was based on a conception that his responsibility for the conduct of foreign affairs and national defense might require some variations in such disposition of these awards that the Civil Aeronautics Board might make. Since 1943, however, the decisions of the Board have been varied by the President in a manner that is definitely indicative of the exercise of power in ways never contemplated by the original Act. Although the approaches to the "White House" are necessarily shrouded in mystery, enough evidence exists to establish the fact that in this particular field "lobbying" in its worst sense was prevalent.

Instances have also recently been uncovered of actual malfeasance in the sense of bribery among high administrative officials. More serious than these are the subtle but pervasive methods pursued by regulated industries to influence regulatory agencies by social favors, promises of later employment in the industry itself, and other similar means.

Malfeasance to some degree will always characterize any human institution. The federal judiciary has not been immune from it. Laws exist which make malfeasance by administrators a crime and in the graver situations convictions of offenders have been obtained. The *ex parte* problem, however, is more insidious and more difficult to cope with. To shut off administrators from contact with the regulated industries except through formal proceedings is to restrict their means of gathering that very expertise that was the reason for the creation of the agency. To shut them off from persons, such as mayors and members of Congress, who are pressing for the public interest as they see it, is to keep them away from a grass roots exploration of what the needs of any segment of the public are. On the other hand, some restraints upon off-the-record approaches must be placed, in view of the fact that the extent of these has grown rather than lessened since World War II. Means of dealing with this problem are suggested in a later section of this report.

E. Administrative Procedures

Administrative procedures and practices have been a constant concern of the agencies themselves, the courts, the bar and scholars for a time long antedating World War II. Pleas for flexibility in these procedures characterized the situation in the early 1930's. Application of even lax rules of evidence to administrative proceedings, particularly when they were being conducted by laymen, was thought undesirable. Commingling of the prosecuting and adjudicatory functions was deemed not only necessary but advisable.

A reaction to these tendencies set in during the latter part of that decade. Records had become unduly long, causing expense and delay. Procedures unchecked by basic require-ments other than loose concepts of due process varied from agency to agency bringing a sense of confusion into the entire administrative process. The combination of the functions of prosecutor and judge, especially in the hands of laymen, developed a belief that elements of fairness were too frequent-ly absent. Courts through their exercise of the power of judicial review sought to remedy some of these matters but the cures suggested frequently only increased the difficulties faced by the agencies in disposing of the business that confronted them.

Beginning about 1938 concerted efforts were made to deal with these problems. At the outset, spurred on by an antago-nism to the very powers exercised by the regulatory agencies, the bar as a whole sought to impose the straight-jacket of traditional judicial procedure on the agencies. They were countered by other forces which sought to retain the value of the administrative process but still advocated reforms that would assure fairness in the exercise of powers delegated to the agencies. Some eight years thereafter a compromise between these two opposing views was effected by the enact-ment of the Administrative Procedure Act of 1946. That Act, however one may evaluate it, is far from a definitive solution of the problem with which it dealt. It has achieved some uniformity of procedure, some assurance of the application of fairer standards, but with its emphasis on "judicialization" has made for delay in the handling of many matters before these agencies.

Revisions and amendments to the Administrative Procedure Act are a constant and continuing concern of both the bar and the government. This is bound to continue and it is good that it should continue. No single mind and no group of minds can in any short period of time grapple with all the complexities of administrative procedure and bring forth a reasonably definitive code. This is a problem which has to be tackled piece by piece and year by year by men who have a continuing concern with its ever-changing phases. No "Hoover Commission" or "Advisory Committee" established other than on a continuing basis can hope to evolve those procedures that should govern the many different problems that the various regulatory agencies face. The traditional concepts themselves are elusive. Rate-making, for example, has as many different facets as a diamond. In the regulation of railroad rates considerations are present that are wholly different from the regulation of rates for electric power or the transmission of gas or oil. Air passenger fares and air freight rates present variant problems due in part to the rapid obsolescence of equipment. Rates for natural gas producers pose an entirely different story. The attempt to analogize these methods through a common concept of a rate of return on invested capital has a more theoretical than realistic basis. Procedures for the discovery of the facts upon which these differing judgments must be made cannot (and should not) necessarily be uniform.

Very recently suggestions have been advanced that due to modern techniques for the assemblage of facts, the older "judicialized" forms may well be supplanted. The exact technology applicable to such a process has not as yet been clearly articulated. But if judgments of regulatory agencies in many fields such as rates are, in truth, business judgments rather than judgments conforming to a legal theory, techniques which do not rest upon the tedious process of examination and cross-examination and which underlie honest business judgments made by the industries may have a value in the handling of substantially the same problem by the agencies. Indeed, in certain areas of transportation, the issue no longer is a fair rate of return on invested capital but how much the traffic can bear since the public interest requires the economic survival of the particular means of transport. Minimal and, perhaps, subsidized rates will be the most recurring issue, rather than the determination of maximal rates which was required in an age of non-competing modes of transportation.

F. Administrative Organization

Akin to the problem of administrative procedure is that of the organization of the regulatory agencies. Various general proposals have been made during the past few years. One of the most radical, recently pressed by a former member of the Civil Aeronautics Board, is a separation of their "policy" functions from the adjudicatory functions. These "policy" functions would be transferred to an executive department, leaving the adjudicatory functions with the commission members. The commission as a body is said to be incapable of policy making since it is required to adopt the wrong procedures, namely quasi-judicial methods, to formulate policy.

Admittedly many of the commissions have neglected their planning or creative functions. This is due in large part to the burden of the routine business thrust upon them and also to the caliber of appointment which have been made in recent years. Planning and policy making have, however, on occasion been carried on effectively by commissions. The specialist study by the Securities and Exchange Commission, its unlisted trading study, its examination of corporate reorganization, its investment company study, its examination of corporate trustees, the public utility holding company study of the Federal Trade Commission, its basing point study, the international route study of the Civil Aeronautics Board, are all examples of effective studies and planning undertaken by commissions all of which have eventuated in basic national policies. "Policy" is also formulated in the process of decision making as witness the differentiation of private versus public offerings of securities or the contrasting roles of trunk and local service carriers. Decision making, however, throws up issues less rarely as a result of deliberate planning and most frequently as a result of the incidence or accidence of cases or controversies. Policy also emanates from rule-making where forward-planning is more possible as, for example, the current effort of the Securities and Exchange Commission to fit so-called variable annuities into the existing pattern of regulation of financial mechanisms designed to absorb the people's savings.

The real issue is not whether the planning function should be delegated to an executive or to a commission but whether the individuals entrusted with such a responsibility have the capacity and the time with which to discharge it. A subsidiary issue is whether the individuals to whom such a function is entrusted are free to use flexible procedures in the search for ideas and policies, or are bound either as a matter of routine or law to pursue procedures ill-adapted for the performance of such a function. In both respects many of our commissions suffer. On the other hand, they can bring to the process of planning a wealth of information and knowledge based upon their experience and their realization of the practical limits of administrative action. These qualities are important as contrasted with planning functions performed in the isolation of an ivory tower.

Some functions that are more truly planning than adjudicatory have been forced too rigidly into the latter mould. This is true of the grant of air line certificates, of licenses for radio and TV transmission, of the reorganization and recapitalization of utility holding companies, of the issuance of pipe line certificates and of rate making in general. The cure here is not the transfer of these functions to an executive department but the adoption and initiation of procedures more suited to deal with the problems they present.

Indeed, some such transfers of these functions have not proved to be too successful. No policy, not even a discernible pattern, has emerged from the President's handling of international air routes and air carriers. Considerable controversy attends the promulgation of rules by the one-man Federal Aviation Agency without following procedures that admit of participation by the various segments of the industry in their formulation. The planning now centered in the General Counsel of the National Labor Relations Board by virtue of his control over the initiation of complaints, has in the opinion of many observers been more of a hit and miss operation than a comprehensive and cohesive approach to a difficult problem.

Generalizations as to the organization of administrative agencies are not only difficult but dangerous to make. One generalization, however, can safely be made. Unlike the judges of the federal judiciary, members of administrative commissions do not do their own work. The fact is that they simply cannot do it. In adjudicatory matters, the drafting of opinions is delegated to opinion writing sections or assistants so that the rationalization upon which a purportedly informed decision rests is not truly their own. One can well imagine the morass which would characterize our Constitutional law dealing with "due process" had the Justices of the Supreme Court for the last half century bad their opinions drafted by clerks and issued anonymously. Who could then assay the work or the philosophy of a Holmes, a Brandeis, a Hughes or a Cardozo? Yet, this is substantially the state of the law emanating from the thousands of decisions issued by the Civil Aeronautics Board, the Interstate Commerce Commission, the Securities and Exchange Commission, the Federal Power Commission and the National Labor Relations Board. But worse than this, it is a general belief, founded on considerable evidence, that briefs of counsel, findings of hearing examiners, relevant portions of the basic records, are rarely read by the individuals theoretically responsible for the ultimate decision. It is difficult for them to do otherwise, for as the analysis of the work load of one commissioner indicated, he had to make a decision during his work-day every five minutes, or as another commissioner recently testified, he made 18,000 decisions in five years. The fact is that delegation on a wide scale, not patently recognized by the law, characterizes the work of substantially all the regulatory agencies and certainly all the major ones. Absent such delegation, the work of these agencies would grind to a stop.

The real issue that we face is whether to recognize openly this fact of delegation or continue with the present facade of non-delegation, which prevents administrators from doing the work for which they have been appointed. There are answers to this problem as will be indicated later but they entail broad changes in the presuppositions that the public has been led to believe underlies the work of our regulatory agencies.

James M. Landis

Apart from this generalization and its implications, it is unsafe to speculate broadly upon the appropriate organization of the regulatory agencies. The architectural design fit for a railroad station may be totally unfit for an air line terminal and certainly unusable as a marine dockyard. There are, of course, stresses and strains in any structure and the mathematical laws governing their computation are uniform, but the agencies have to be shaped internally for the functions that they are intended to serve. The Bureau of the Budget has in recent years engaged a series of management consultant firms to make studies of the major agencies at a cost of some $290,000. These studies vary greatly in quality and may be criticized on the ground that their conclusions lack a certain degree of independence. Since these consultants are presumably experts in the esoteric art of management rather than experts in the field covered by the agency or in administrative procedures, they are limited in their scope to the management side of the agencies rather than being concerned with the substantive character of their operations. Whether a hearing examiner spends two days or two months in the preparation of his findings is less important than the quality of the final product and that quality is not measurable by mechanical means.

These management studies are of varying quality and disparate value. They may in some situations ease bottlenecks and streamline the operations of departments that have become mired in outworn routines. It is, perhaps, too early to assess the impact of these studies. There is considerable opinion that the Howrey "reorganization" of the Federal Trade Commission, following the lines recommended by the management consultants and contrary to those recommended by the Hoover Commission in 1950, has been productive of delay rather than expedition. Also the concept of the executive director, which has been adopted by some of the commissions and which runs through most of these reports, has yet to become crystallized and prove itself. A chief assistant to a chairman, provided that the chairman has the responsibility to handle the administrative aspects of the agency's work, seems less presumptuous and appears to work better. Persons with grandiose titles tend to assume grandiose powers and forget that a chairman with respect to his colleagues and almost as much with respect to important departmental heads must give the impression that he is *primus* but only *inter pares*.

Follow-up surveys should, of course, be conducted to determine what recommendations have been adopted and proved themselves as well as what recommendations have been rejected. The responsibility of the Bureau of the Budget in this respect should not be sporadic but continuing and should itself make some evaluation of the recommendations submitted by the management consultants.

G. The Formulation of Policy Within the Agency

A prime criticism of the regulatory agencies is their failure to develop broad policies in the areas subject to their jurisdiction. As this report noted earlier policy formulation can be made in various ways including the adjudicatory process. The failure to utilize other methods for policy formulation is due primarily to the pressure of business on the adjudicatory side.

"Policy formulation", unless required by the disposition of a particular case, means planning measures as how best to dispose of pending problems or how best to forecast and exploit solutions to problems still on the horizon. In the former field there are outstanding failures such as the allocation problem in the television field and rate regulation of natural gas producers. A series of other hiatuses in various regulatory fields can be mentioned, arising out of the inability to fashion viable patterns through the process of adjudication. Thus, the licensing of television and radio stations forms no decipherable pattern to permit the adjudicatory process to be both fairly and relatively easily exercised. The certification of air carriers on particular routes presents the same picture. Enforcement of the Robinson-Patman Act, due to the vagaries of the basic legislation, suffers from the same fault. In areas such as these where the case-by-case method has failed to prick out decipherable patterns and create "policies," other methods of policy planning are required.

Where, however, the greatest gaps exist are in the planning for foreseeable problems. Absent such planning the need for *ad hoc* solutions to the particular manifestations of the problem precede and, indeed, may preclude any basic policy formulation. The duty to undertake such planning is set forth with considerable specificity in many of the basic statutes creating the agencies, and yet plans have failed to evolve. Transportation is the most obvious of these areas. Planning to deal with the inevitable impact of increased competition on both long-haul and short-haul freight and passenger rail transportation has been minimal. Bureaucratic obstacles to the abandonment of unprofitable inter-city service became so severe and so unrealistic that the Transportation Act of 1958 sought in a way, perhaps too severely, to cut the Gordian knot. The problems of the shorter-haul carrier, such as the New Haven Railroad, could be seen long in advance but plans to deal with the problem as such have not yet been devised. The general deterioration of rail service, particularly on the Eastern roads, goes on apace, yet its tie-in with rates and financing is still to be determined. Such solutions as have been devised are piecemeal in character and bold and imaginative thinking is lacking. Commodity tariff classifications still reflect an economy whose changes have made many of them obsolete. In aviation much the same is occurring. The impact of the jet plane, substantially tripling the capacity of propeller-driven aircraft on our domestic and international route structures has received no serious consideration despite the obvious threat that the advent of the jet poses for the position of many of our intermediate trunk carriers. Instead of forward route planning the CAB now finds itself faced with potential mergers that under the pressure of financial exigency may force changes in route patterns and route structures far different from those that might otherwise have been deemed desirable. With planes with a Mach 2 speed already on the drawing boards planning far beyond the now conventional jet is necessary. Re-evaluation of our theories of international air rights and routes should similarly be now in process. In the maritime field, due to new competitive forces and the changing patterns of world commerce, re-examination must constantly be made of our subsidy policies which may be producing uneconomic competition on over-expanded trade routes in foreign commerce. Indeed, the impact of subsidy in many fields calls for re-examination of existing goals. Until World War II, the conception of the airplane as a commercial transport was limited to passengers and mail. Its adaptation, particularly since the advent of the jet, to extensive air cargo operations may well be more valuable from a national standpoint than the $60,000,000 to $80,000,000 now being paid annually to keep our local service airlines alive. Time spent on a problem such as this can well be more rewarding to the public interest than on an issue as to whether cities X and Y should be interlinked by more passenger air service.

James M. Landis

H. Inter-Agency Policy Formulation

If there is lack of policy formulation within agencies, there is an almost complete barrenness of such formulation for those matters with which groups of agencies are concerned. The few inter-agency committees that have been set up have accomplished too little in conducting their separate approaches to a common problem. The most successful, the Air Coordinating Committee, proved so unsuccessful in dealing with the major problem of air space control that its function in this respect had to be turned over by the Federal Aviation Act of 1958 to a single agency, the Federal Aeronautics Administration.

There are many areas calling for well coordinated attacks upon problems common to many agencies. This is true in the fields of transportation, communications, energy, monopoly, and unfair trade practices. The development of a national transportation policy, as urged in the Democratic platform of 1960, calls for the achievement of maximum efficiency in transport, which, in turn means that "at a given level and structure of capital Investment efficiency requires that traffic be distributed among motor carriers, railroads, water carriers, pipelines and air carriers in such a way that each type receives the traffic which it can carry with the best consumption of resources by the carrier for the service standards required by the user. It requires also that several forms of transport be used in coordination where such a combination can produce a better service-cost result than any single form working alone. Finally it requires that every enterprise participating be ably and energetically managed." See Williams and Bluestone. *Federal Transportation Policy and Program*, p. 2.

The prime Federal Agencies concerned with the development of such a policy are the ICC, the CAB, the FMB, the FPC, the

Bureau of Public Roads, the Military Transportation Service, the Army Corps of Engineers and the Department of Commerce. With reference to some phases of transportation it will also become necessary to effect coordination with various state and municipal agencies in order to deal with problems of a local or regional nature.

The inability to effect inter-agency coordination has been responsible for the lack of any policy as to the nature of the competition that should exist as between forms of transportation and also as between the carriers themselves. Military transportation, as presently conducted, competes heavily with commercial transportation, and there are patent abuses that attach to the government as a mass shipper, but it still insists on going its own way regardless of the effects its policies may have upon other carriers. Improvement of our rivers continues at the expense of the railroads, who are given the dubious privilege of reducing their rates to meet this new competition. The commutation crisis that was apparent a decade ago has had little or no effective help from the Federal Government despite some rather casual and ineffectual investigations by the Interstate Commerce Commission. The only remedy thus far devised has been periodic increases in commutation rates, a seemingly endless process since the causes that make for deterioration remain unchecked. Despite the tremendous decreases in rail passenger movements and their increasing costs the defeatist observation of the Interstate Commerce Commission examiners to this general problem to the effect that the passenger railroad car is likely to be found only in a museum in the 1970's is not likely to become true. User charges based upon use of federal facilities or federally subsidized facilities are unevenly distributed among the various forms of transportation thus favoring one form of transportation as against another, and imposing upon the taxpayer costs properly chargeable to others.

It is unnecessary to catalog further the many different areas of interaction and the achievements that might be accomplished were an articulate national transportation policy to be ground out by the process of coordination. Thus strengthening our transportation system for peacetime purposes means much for it can that much more effectively respond to wartime needs.

Communications presents a second area where effective interagency action is lacking. Present communication policy making machinery was established in 1934 in the context of regulating a private industry, and before the advent of radar, television, jet aircraft, intercontinental rockets, space communications and radio astronomy. Since then new demands from industry, new needs in international telecommunication and new means of communication have created a situation where the coordination of various endeavors must be effectuated if we would deal with communications effectively in the national interest. This is particularly true in the cold war environment of the 1960's which calls upon us to utilize every resource available in the telecommunications field in our struggle not merely for prestige but for survival.

Many agencies have a concern with the problems in this area. They include the Federal Communications Commission, the State Department, the National Aeronautics and Space Administration, the Interdepartmental Radio Advisory Committee of the Office of Civil and Defense Mobilization, the Army, the Navy, the Air Force, and the Federal Aeronautics Administration. The problems are many and complex. They involve the allocation of both radio and television frequencies as between Federal and non-Federal uses — an allocation that has not been satisfactorily solved and whose present solution entails increasing difficulties in the international field as new nations, presently neutrals but hopefully our allies, are pressing for frequencies in the high frequency band for domestic communications and to express their personalities on the air waves of the world. Redistribution of spectrum space internationally is almost certainly in the offing and its effect upon our vital communication facilities, both Federal and non-Federal, must be considered. Modern developments in space telecommunications, as set forth in two reports dated March 19, 1960, and December 4, 1960, to the Senate Committee on Aeronautical and Space Sciences point up the possibilities of substantial augmentation of our presently limited intercontinental communications through communication satellites, thus relieving our present dependence on the limited high frequency band. Mechanisms for the effective exploration and utilization of this augmented spectrum must be developed in an atmosphere far broader than that allotted to and operable by any single existing agency. Only a closely coordinated combination of the appropriate agencies concerned with this problem can make such mechanisms possible.

The necessary coordination today is non-existent. The Federal Communications Commission expends substantially all its energies on the handling of problems relating to public broadcasting. The Telecommunications Division within the State Department entrusted with international telecommunication relationships is several layers deep within the Department. It has been permitted to decline in expertness, leadership, activity in international matters, as well as personnel. The International Radio Advisory Committee has a responsibility with reference to Federal and non-Federal frequency allocations but each government body makes its own allocations within the areas allotted to it, so that apportionment of the radio spectrum is a matter of *ad hoc* negotiation rather than of planned usage. There exists also a Presidential telecommunications adviser whose many other duties frequently overshadow telecommunications. Other committees are advisory to executive departments or offices such as the Telecommunications Coordinating Committee, the Telecommunications Advisory Board and the Telecommunications Planning Committee. But no general over-all coordination exists out of which broad national policies can emerge.

Studies pointing up the lack of this coordination and suggesting various means to cure that lack have been carried on for some 10 years. Bills to create a new authority with wide powers have been introduced from time to time in the Congress, and have generally met severe opposition from the Executive Department. Hearings upon a similar bill introduced this year have already evoked the strong opposition of the Department of Defense.

Energy is another area where interaction is essential and where substantially none exists. If we would increase our energy resources and utilize them wisely, coordination both as to utilization and conservation is essential. Various departments and agencies have a concern with segments of this problem. Surface transportation of oil, coal and liquefied gas lies within the purview of the Interstate Commerce Commission and the Federal Maritime Board, and surface transportation of fuels is of enormous consequence in view of the importance of transportation costs in the pricing of the product. Natural gas is a concern of the Federal Power Commission. Electric power in its various forms falls within the purview of the Federal Power Commission, the Department of the Interior, the Corps of Army Engineers, the Tennessee Valley Authority and similar entities. The derivation of energy from fissionable materials is the business of the Atomic Energy Commission. General concern over the conservation of resources from which energy is developed rests primarily with the Department of the interior, whereas the State Department and the Tariff Commission are factors in dealing with the extent to which our foreign investment is concerned with the production of fuel abroad as well as the extent to which these fuels should enter the domestic market.

Government actually controls to a considerable extent the degree to which these fuels are competitive and the exercise of these controls can affect to a great degree the rate of consumption of our resources. Indeed, the rate at which our own resources of natural gas are being tapped to a point where within a foreseeable period they may be exhausted is, in the opinion of many, a worrisome problem. But the coordination of policies with regard to their use and their conservation has not developed; indeed, an over-all concern with these questions has hardly been evidenced.

Perhaps more important than this is the matter of the continued development of other sources of energy. In this area the hydrogenation of coal and oil-bearing rock is outstanding. In the opinion of many an all-out national effort similar to that which has harnessed atomic energy might well solve this problem in such a way that we might not need to concern ourselves with sources of energy for another hundred years. But inter-agency mechanisms for planning or even suggesting such projects are absent.

Still other areas point up the need for coordination or the elimination of overlapping jurisdictions. Chief among these are the areas of monopoly and unfair trade practices. In the former the Federal Trade Commission and the Department of

Justice have an overlapping jurisdiction, although they employ different sanctions to achieve their results. Some concern with the problems of monopoly are also the concern of the Interstate Commerce Commission, the Civil Aeronautics Board, the Federal Power Commission and the Federal Communications Commission. The sanctions possessed by the Department of Justice appear over the years to be more effective and more expeditious than are employed by the Federal Trade Commission. In the field of unfair trade practices, particularly false advertising, there is also an overlap between the Federal Trade Commission and the Food and Drug Administration now under the Department of Health, Education and Welfare. Efforts to resolve this jurisdictional conflict were undertaken without success in 1933-1934 and have intermittently been tackled since. A possibility of conflict also exists in the field of insecticides and fertilizers between the Food and Drug Administration and the Department of Agriculture, subsidiary phases of which recently came to light during the recent notable cranberry episode. Jurisdictional lines inevitably dim at different points, but where the overlapping jurisdictions are patent, concurrent and uncoordinated regulation can evolve differing policies as well as produce unnecessary expense and bureaucratic waste.

I. The Relationship of the Agencies to the Executive

The relationship of the agencies to the Executive has never been appropriately defined. It probably cannot be, but the shadows that now surround it can to a degree be lifted. In this respect there is not too great a difference between the allegedly "independent" agencies and those technically a part of some Executive Department. The President's arbitrary interference with the operations of the Commodity Exchange Administration would be subject to resentment equal to that engendered by a similar interference with the Securities and Exchange Commission. The same would hold whether it involved Food and Drug Administration or the Federal Trade Commission. Whatever relationship can be spelled out as appropriate for the independent agencies, such a relationship would *a fortiori* hold for the other agencies.

The independent agencies are clearly dependent upon the Executive in four respects. The first is, of course, in the matter of appointments at the commissioner level. The degree to which they are subject to removal at the pleasure of the President is not uniformly clear. Where the statute prohibits their removal except for cause the President's power of removal is limited to "cause". *Humphrey's Executor v. United States*, 195 U. S. 602 (1934). But there is no suggestion as to the extent to which judicial review could be had over a finding of "cause" by the President. Where no such prohibitions exist in the statute, a similar limitation may, however, be read into the statute for appointees who exercise quasi-judicial duties. Cf. *Wiener v. United States*, 357 U. S. 349 (1958).

A second definite relationship exists between these agencies and the President in that the Bureau of the Budget controls the budget submitted by the agency to the Congress and the agency is expected to support this budget. This does not mean that the Congress may not appropriate sums to the agency in excess of those approved by the Bureau, but in practice such over-appropriations are rare. The President thus through his practical control over agency expenditures can affect vary substantially the emphasis placed by the agency on certain of its activities.

A third relationship arises out of the fact, now generally acknowledged although at one time contested by Commissioner Eastman of the Interstate Commerce Commission, that no legislative proposal shall be submitted by the independent agencies to the Congress unless they have been cleared through the Bureau of the Budget. This restriction also applies to other than casual comments made by the agency on bills pending before the Congress.

The fourth relationship arises out of the fact that, except for the Interstate Commerce Commission, the President appoints from among the agency members a chairman with more or less general administrative power. The situation with respect to the Federal Power Commission is somewhat confused in this respect due to a palpable error in the drafting of the reorganization plan covering that agency. The appointed chairman presumably is the avenue of contact between the agency and the President although this has not always been the case.

Other less tangible relationships exist. For some years now the Bureau of the Budget has concerned itself with the administrative management of the various major agencies. This concern has grown in recent years to the point where the Bureau has engaged outside managerial consultants to survey the major agencies. Subsequent surveillance as to the effectiveness of these surveys in bringing about managerial improvements is being undertaken. The Bureau of the Budget is thus quietly and unassumingly becoming in essence a Bureau of Administrative Management, to the functions of which it could, if it so chose, attach powerful sanctions.

Consultations may occur with more but usually with less frequency between the President and the chairman or members of the agency. The absence of national politics pricked out by the agencies and the complexity involved in the handling of any national problem due to its Balkanization among a series of agencies makes worthwhile consultations of this type rare and consequently infrequent. A device has thus grown up in the past two administrations of delegating these agency and inter-agency problems to one or more "White House assistants". This procedure has had its shortcomings. These assistants have either not had the knowledge or the prestige to be effective in handling agency chairmen and members, especially those in the "independent" category; or, if the assistant possesses the prestige sufficient to qualify him popularly as an "Assistant President" he tends to overstep the bounds of his authority and tends to interfere in the disposition by the agency of individual cases. A reference to the interference of Sherman Adams in the Dixon-Yates matter or to the Murray (Chotiner) — Sherm (Adams) correspondence in the North American Airlines case pending before the Civil Aeronautics Board is sufficient to illustrate this point.

There is an obvious necessity for the President to keep abreast of such national policies as may or may not be in the making or the handling or failure to handle national problems of national impact. He has also the constitutional duty to see that the laws are faithfully executed and this duty is applicable to the execution of laws entrusted to regulatory agencies, whether technically "independent" or not. The patent failure of the Federal Power Commission to execute the laws relating to natural gas production is thus rightly a matter of constitutional concern to him. As to this failure the Circuit Court of Appeals of the District of Columbia recently on December 8, 1960, had this to say:

"We believe that the Supreme Court [in the *Catco* case] meant to impress upon the Commission an interpretation of the "public interest" which, in the context of a rising natural gas market, demands a real administrative effort to hold back prices. We find nothing in the record before us which would justify the conclusion that the Commission had adequately performed this duty."

Whether such failure adequately to perform a statutory duty would be "cause" for removal is a question as to which lawyers might argue but which from the practical governmental standpoint permits of only one answer.

The congestion of the dockets of the agencies, the delays incident to the disposition of cases, the failure to evolve policies pursuant to basic statutory requirements are all a part of the President's constitutional concern to see that the laws are faithfully executed. The outcome of any particular adjudicatory matter is, however, as much beyond his concern, except where he has a statutory responsibility to intervene, as the outcome of any cause pending in the courts and his approach to such matters before the agencies should be exactly the same as his approach to matters pending before the courts.

Delegation of his constitutional responsibilities in this area is obviously essential, but, on the basis of past experience the device of one or more "White Rouse assistants" is not the answer.

J. Relationship of the Agencies to the Legislative

The relationship of the agencies to the Congress generally speaking is that of any statutory branch of the Executive to the Congress, with certain exceptions. Oversight of their activities is naturally a concern of the Congress. But with respect to their quasi-judicial functions they should have the same immunity as courts. This does not mean that the Congress should not inquire into any improprieties in their quasi-judicial behavior. In this respect the opportunity of inquiry is, perhaps, greater than with respect to federal judges, but, given no impropriety, the rationality of their decisions or their attitude towards the handling of pending causes, even though some of them may not yet have reached the adjudicatory stage, should not be subject to inquiry. Their independence in this respect should be as much respected as that of the judges.

Their responsibility is to the Congress rather than solely to the Executive. The policies that they are supposed to pursue are those that have been delineated by the Congress not by the Executive. Departure from these policies or the failure to make them effective or their subordination of legislative goals to the directions of the Executive is thus a matter of necessary legislative concern.

There is no question but that Congress has both the right and duty to inquire into effectiveness of the operation of the regulatory agencies and their handling of the broad powers that have been delegated to them. The real issue is the capacity of the Congress to keep abreast of the programs and the policies being carried out by these agencies.

In this respect Congress is faced with the same difficulties that attach to the Executive, namely the need to delegate its responsibilities in the face of other demands on its time and the difficulties of evaluating the basic national problems involved because of the many agencies dealing with them. The agencies touch the Congress, at least at two points — the Appropriations Committee and the appropriate committee, such as the Committees on Interstate and Foreign Commerce, having jurisdiction over their subject matter. Since the Legislative Reorganization Act of 1946, these committees have been furnished with better and more competent staffs. This is a definite help and enables the Committee to pierce the self-serving testimony normally adduced from the agencies. Relatively substantial improvement has thus occurred in this field, but more is needed. The committee staffs are often not too competent or have such short lives that they cannot become too familiar with the complex problems facing the major agencies. It is not easy quickly to evaluate the competency and efficiency of any particular agency especially when its activities fail to give an integrated picture.

Usually these investigations or hearings are sporadic in nature having been sparked by some incident that has caught the attention of the press. Regular surveys of their activities would be far more valuable. Usually their annual reports, always too self-serving, suggest some change in their basic statutes and this request for legislative aid gives a good ground for a survey of their past record. Annual or even biennial committee examination, based upon thorough prior preparation, would permit the Congress to have a better knowledge of the caliber of their personnel and the manner in which they are discharging their responsibilities.

II. SUGGESTED REMEDIES

These then are the major problems that face our growingly important scheme of administrative regulation. It is not possible to deal with all these problems either administratively, by executive action or by legislation. They will require the use of every method, but executive action promises more expeditious handling of many of them. The fact is that during the last decade the Executive appears to have had no real concern with their operation. True, beginnings have been made to survey their capacity to manage their business, in keeping track of their operations through the accumulation of statistics by the establishment of an office of Administrative Procedure in the Department of Justice, in stimulating conferences on administrative procedure, in studying some of the elements essential to the development of a national transportation policy, and in advancing the career service of the hearing examiners. But such advances have been nullified by the appointment of members of these agencies on political grounds, and by not advancing to posts of significance within the agencies men experienced by long service in their business. Largely on political grounds, outsiders lacking necessary qualification for their important tasks have been appointed. There has also been too much of the morale-shattering practice of permitting executive interference in the disposition of causes and controversies delegated to the agencies for decision. Never before recent times in the history of the administrative process have the federal courts been compelled to return administrative decisions to the agencies, not because they have erred, but because they have departed from those fundamentals of ethics that must characterize equally the performance of quasi-judicial and judicial duties. Cancers such as these sweep through the entire process dulling the sense of public service and destroying the confidence that the public must repose in public servants.

A. Delay, Costs and Agency Organization

Some of the causes of delay with its concomitant increase of costs have been set forth above. The existing state of the organization of many of the agencies is one chief reason for their delays. Their re-organization to correct this situation is thus essential and can be accomplished best and most expeditiously by the Executive. His constitutional responsibility to see that the laws are faithfully executed calls upon him to do so. The Executive, moreover, is less beset by the vested interests in bureaucracy that too often find support from members of the Congress. To do this, however, he must be empowered to act.

The first step consequently is, at least, to revive powers heretofore granted the President under the Reorganization Act of 1949, under which the power of the President to submit reorganization plans expired on June 1, 1959. A simple statute can do this. It would be better, however, in view of the bureaucratic pressures that are capable of being organized, as was evidenced by the defeat of President Truman's Plan No. 7 for the reorganization of the Interstate Commerce Commission, to require that the veto powers by the Congress over reorganization plans submitted by the President should require a majority in both Houses of Congress. The leadership of the President in these matters should be respected by the Congress unless he is palpably wrong.

Blueprints as to further reorganization of the various agencies cannot be submitted at this time. But certain ideas as to what the outlines of each reorganization should generally be can be suggested. These can best be set forth by a brief examination of some of the major regulatory agencies.

1. The Interstate Commerce Commission

Among the agencies principally calling for reorganization is the Interstate Commerce Commission. It lacks positive direction because of the absence of the position of a chairman who is other than a presiding officer. The theory of a rotating chairman, elected annually by the membership, may assuage the ambitions of its membership, but it deprives the Commission of that leadership that it so sadly needs. The informed public generally knows the names of the heads of our Executive Departments and has some sense of the general policies that they advocate. But even the informed public within the railroad and trucking industries have no idea and care less who, for the time being, might be the Chairman of the Interstate Commerce Commission. The selection of the Chairman from among its membership is essential but it is equally essential that he be appointed to that office by the President and hold it at his pleasure. A chairman must evince an ability to manage the mechanism over which he presides so that delays and unnecessary bureaucratic procedures do not characterize its work. He must be able to obtain the respect and loyalty of his colleagues and, above all, take the lead in the formulation of the policies that the Commission should pursue. His powers should include the appointment of all personnel to the agency, save the heads of the prime Divisions or Bureaus where the assent of his colleagues can be required and also reserving to his colleagues certain excepted positions necessary to enable them to perform their individual tasks. He should have complete authority as to the internal organization of the agency, the divisions and bureaus into which it should be divided, and the complete responsibility, subject to the review of the Bureau of the Budget, for its budget. He should also be the spokesman for the agency before the Congress, the President, and the Executive Departments, although he naturally would advise with his colleagues on such matters as well as delegate to others matters that he believes can be better handled by them. He should not, however, restrict the free expression of views differing from his by his colleagues to the Congress, the President or the public.

Such a change would permit the centralization of responsibility for the operations of the agency in a manner whereby its operations can be far more easily evaluated by the Congress, the President and the public. Moreover, the position would then attach to itself a prestige equal to that of a Cabinet post, which it now plainly lacks. Nor would this change detract from the responsibilities and prestige of the other members for, by relieving them of their present multitudinous administrative duties, they could devote themselves, which they physically cannot do at the present time, to a personal consideration of the problems before them. It may be contended that such an arrangement would destroy the "independence" of the agency. This would not, however, be the fact, for the failure of the Chairman to retain the confidence and respect of his colleagues would create a situation justifying the President in replacing him by some other member competent to assume these responsibilities.

The membership of the Interstate Commerce Commission, eleven in number and the largest of any regulatory agency, gives ground for concern. Commissioners have been added to the Interstate Commerce Commission from time to time on the theory that their addition was necessary because of the increased work load of the Commission. The Commission was authorized to create panels of three or more members to dispose of cases before it, and it has done so. However, the right to get a reconsideration of a panel decision by the full Commission has been so broad that reconsiderations of panel decisions are very frequently requested and too frequently granted. Reforms in this panel process of decision must be made so that rarely will the unwieldy number of eleven Commissioners be called on as a body to determine issues generally never more consequential than those finally disposed of by three judges in our Circuit Courts of Appeal.

Opinions of the Interstate Commerce Commission are presently in the poorest category of all administrative agency opinions. Their source is unknown and the practice has grown up of parsimony in discussing the applicable law in making a determination. Lengthy recitals of the contentions of the various parties are made as a prelude to a succinct conclusion devoid of real rationalization. This practice was inveighed against by a distinguished former member, Commissioner Aitcheson, but it has not been changed. The creation of an opinion writing section has been urged by the managerial consultants hired to survey the Commission. But opinion writing sections are not the answer even at their best as in the Securities and Exchange Commission. Individual Commissioners must be assigned the responsibility of expressing the conclusions of the Commission. They will, of course, need help and appropriate help in the nature of law clerks such as are now assigned to federal judges, rather than the present practice of temporarily assigning attorneys from the staff of a Bureau. Law clerks personally attached to a Commissioner will take pride in their chief's performance just as the law clerks seek now to perfect the work of their judges.

The individual commissioners are presently assigned administrative duties as supervisors of various Bureaus within the Commission. This is unnecessary and disruptive of the time of the Commissioners.

A major problem in the reorganization of the Interstate Commerce Commission, as in most other agencies, is the delegation of appropriate duties to persons below the Commission level. Some advance in this respect has been made by the organization of four employee boards to deal with a series of non-hearing cases from whose decisions an appeal can be made to the Commission. In hearing cases the decision can be carried to the full 40 Commission level by exceptions directly from the hearing examiner's report or upon a request for reconsideration of a decision by a panel of Commissioners. Delegation of matters to a greater degree than this is admittedly made difficult by specific provisions of the Interstate Commerce Act which, more than any of the other basic statutes, defines the procedural requirements to be followed by the Commission. However, changes even in these procedural requirements could seemingly be effected by Presidential action under the Reorganization Act provided that no infringement is made upon the right of judicial review.

Whether a reorganization plan could make final the decisions by single Commissioners, hearing examiners, or employee boards in certain groups of cases might be debatable, but a reorganization plan could make them final subject to review akin to the selective review by certiorari now employed as the means by which the Supreme Court of the United States determines which decisions of the Circuit Courts of Appeal it wishes to review. A judicious use of such a scheme and an insistence on brief petitions for certiorari by counsel would cut down enormously the business demanding attention at the Commission level. The legality of such a plan under the concepts of due process is not truly questionable.

Even within the confines of the existing law marked improvement in the manner of handling the adjudicatory problems could be made. The single Commissioner technique is rarely, if ever, utilized. Replacing a panel of three by a single Commissioner would obviously conserve a portion of the time of two Commissioners.

Again, the problem of hearing examiners has been handled badly by the Interstate Commerce Commission. The Civil Service classification of some examiners are below those of examiners in the other major agencies. They are regularly assigned to particular Bureaus and are thus confined both in interest and outlook. They have been subjected to the indignity of time clock controls. They have neither secretaries nor other assistants to aid them and frequently are ill-housed. Their reports are also too frequently rewritten for no discernible purpose.

Other reorganizations of the functions of the Commission as well as the tightening and refining of its procedural rules can be effected without the need of a reorganization "plan", and would undoubtedly be effected by an energetic and competent chairman. Suggestions along these lines are contained in the Booz, Allen & Hamilton Report and in the valuable recent Report of the Special Advisory Committee to the Interstate Commerce Commission.

2. The Civil Aeronautics Board

The chief criticisms of the Civil Aeronautics Board center about (1) the inordinate delay in its disposition of proceedings, especially in route cases; (2) the fact that its procedures are such as to make extraordinarily complex the issues before it in various types of proceedings; (3) the intrusion of influences off the record that appear to be determinative of pending cases; (4) a failure to do forward planning of the type necessary to promote our air commerce to its desired level of efficiency.

The inordinate delay in its disposition of pending causes and the complexity of these proceedings arises out of the procedures it applies to them. Issues with regard to route extensions, new routes, and new services come before it for determination as a result of the filing of applications by carriers or would-be carriers. The disposition of these matters pursues no pattern or plan. The result is that issues with regard to the desirability of new routes and new services are commingled with issues as to what carriers should fly what routes, calling for a final judgment that has to be based on political, economic, sociological, business and aeronautical considerations. All the issues in such a proceeding are handled by the lengthy process of examining and cross-examining witnesses. This is a wasteful manner of establishing many of the basic facts.

Routes that in the public interest should be flown are capable of being determined without resort to proceedings of this character but as a result of staff studies carried on in a less formal manner. Evidence now being presented in a formal manner as to the needs of various communities for service, as to the community of interest between communities, as to the desirability for increased competition or the existence of sufficient adequate surface transportation, as to the type of service required and the potentiality of generating a sufficient quantum of air traffic, can all be determined beforehand by less legalistic and reasonably scientific methods; leaving for a "judicialized" hearing only the issue as to which of the competing carriers is to be selected for certification on any particular route. If necessary, hearings could be held on the staff study itself, which also could be of a less formal type. In any event, a procedure of this type would shorten these route proceedings immensely and would be likely to produce better route systems than those produced by the existing procedures.

A system somewhat along these lines was applied initially shortly after World War II in establishing our main international air routes and the resulting air route map has proved itself generally successful. True, following the hearings in the international route cases, modifications of the suggested routes were made by the Board and probably modifications of planned routes would result even from the limited hearings indicated above. But the difference between the suggested procedure and that now being employed is that the former employs the technique of planning whereas the latter starts with a map that is a *tabula rasa* and then permits a hodge-podge of routes to be drawn across its face by the applicants from which the Board finally selects a route pattern for reasons that it frequently cannot even articulate.

The problem of mergers should be handled in the same fashion. Mergers where desirable should follow and be considered within the framework of a planned and articulated transportation policy rather than being brought about by the happenstance of the financial difficulties of a carrier or because one carrier is willing to pay a higher price for a certificate than another carrier. Unfortunately, the Board has hamstrung itself so as to prevent this approach by permitting certificates freely given to a carrier by the Government to become a subject of barter in the market and thus be put on the auction block to be sold to the highest bidder for a price which the public is eventually bound to pay.

These suggested procedures would also affect the pattern of *ex parte* presentations. No objection could rightly be made to *ex parte* presentations at the informal stage, presentations that relate to the need or desirability of new air services. Only at the hearing stage where a choice has to be made as between competing applicants do *ex parte* presentations become truly harmful.

The institution of procedures of this type would seemingly require no legislative action. Furthermore, air carriers and air routes are now so plentiful that it might be desirable tempo-rarily to freeze the situation and ponder over the road that has already been traveled in order to determine just what the next turning should be.

Ex parte presentations and the acceptance of unusual hospitalities have bedeviled the Board probably ever since its creation. They seem to have increased in recent years, although their extent is unknown except as some particular incident has brought them to light. Many of the airlines maintain substantial offices in Washington and have attached to them specialists under various titles whose function is primarily to maintain good relations between the airline and the members and staff of the Board. The control of this problem, which seems to have a greater incidence at the Civil Aeronautics Board, the Federal Power Commission and the Federal Communications Commission — agencies with substantial favors to give out — is dealt with elsewhere in this report. But the Civil Aeronautics Board has a special problem arising out of the President's power over international and overseas routes, where no procedure for influencing the President's determination exists except *ex parte* presentations. There is probably no cure for this situation except the self-restraint, that has notably been lacking in the last two administrations, which the President should impose upon himself in limiting his intervention to considerations of foreign policy and national defense.

The lack of planning on the part of the Board stems from the burden of its adjudicatory work. Planning has been so neglected over the past few years that a staff, fit to be called a planning staff, can hardly any longer be said to exist. At every point major issues of policy remain undecided. Cases being dealt with now are already so obsolete that they even fail to raise these issues, so that policy fails to evolve as fast as it should from the adjudicatory process.

Reorganization to make planning possible is a matter of internal organization. The only need for a "plan" within the meaning of the Reorganization Act lies in further increasing the powers granted to the Chairman in 1950 to the full extent herein suggested for the Interstate Commerce Commission and to permit more flexibility in the delegation of those decisions which require no real ratiocination to hearing examiners or to bureau heads subject to a certiorari type of review by the Board. Among these delegable matters are, with rare exceptions, foreign air carrier permits, approval of air carrier agreements, interlocking arrangements and similar matters.

One internal adjustment should be made insofar as negotiations on international routes are concerned. The board as a whole should not participate in such negotiations, though it may well want to consider the nature of the proposals that could be made or that would be acceptable. The actual negotiations should be headed by one member assisted by a small staff and such representatives as the State Department might choose to take part in a particular negotiation. This would make both for a better negotiating atmosphere, the centralization of responsibility, and the conservation of the time of the other members of the Board.

3. The Securities and Exchange Commission

The problems of the Securities and Exchange Commission are relatively simple. Much of the delays that characterize its operation stem from the fact that it, more than any other agency, has been starved for appropriations. Even the recent increases have not restored the amounts formerly available. What has been responsible for this attitude other than pure ignorance as to the significance of its functions is difficult to fathom. But more than increasing its appropriations is necessary.

Much of the delay that attends the registration of securities could be eliminated by providing for simpler forms of registration and a simplified supervision of the process of registration with respect to seasoned securities, bonds and debentures with an A or B rating and preferred stocks that for a past period have shown an appropriate ratio of earnings to dividends payable on such stocks. In the case of seasoned securities of this nature, the issuer and underwriter should be relied on to furnish full and accurate statements of fact and deficiency letters could be substantially abolished. It could also relieve from registration requirements certain admittedly technical public offerings for which registration is now technically necessary. The necessity for maintaining a currently effective registration statement on convertible securities, options and warrants, when an adequate market exists for the basic securities and adequate information is available in annual financial reports or proxy statements, is an example of a situation where registration is unnecessary. The issuance of restricted options to groups of employees not too excessive in number is another such example. More of them can be found. Relieving the Commission and the industry of the necessity for acting on registration statements in such situations would clear the Commission's docket to some degree and relieve the industry of unnecessary costs.

The deficiency letter, a most valuable extra-legal development, has a real place with regard to the more promotional and speculative securities. There has grown up over the years a considerable tendency to indulge in lint-picking in these letters, resulting in delays and unnecessary costs. Another tendency has become noticeable due to the attitude of certain

Commissioners shortly following World War II. This is to move away from the legislative standards of full disclosure to a judgment on the quality of the securities being registered. The history of state security regulation in this respect gives ample evidence of the undesirability of establishing a bureaucracy with powers of this nature. True, there is every temptation to move in this direction as one views as a whole the rapacity of promoters and underwriters and the unwillingness of a greedy and speculative public to try to understand the simplest facts of corporate finance. But control and supervision over the activities of the selling group and the marginal fringe of brokers and dealers making markets in these issues, can do more to dampen this type of financial piracy than the use of the registration powers for purposes for which it was not intended.

Similarly controls should be extended more widely as against so-called investment advisers, many of whom have morals not exceeding those of tipsters at the race track. Even our con- servative newspapers carry horrendous advertisements as to the prowess of particular advisers and the aura that these advisers have engendered has led to imitation of their tactics by large and respectable brokerage houses. Here is a field that the Securities and Exchange Commission is beginning to plough and money made available for such a purpose will pay ample dividends in turning savings away from rank specula- tion to reasonable investment.

One serious feature of delay on the part of the Securities and Exchange Commission lies in the issuance of regulations and forms. Important regulations have been delayed for years. Some reason for this delay lies in the inherent complexities of the problems and the commendable practice of the Securities and Exchange Commission, so different from that of the

Federal Aviation Agency, of affording opportunities to the industry to comment on proposed regulations. But an element of delay arises from the incapacity of the Commissioners themselves to grasp the essence of these problems and the significance of their resolution to the financial community. Because of the excellence of its staff and the inherent complexities of the problems, the Commission in a sense is the captive of its staff. It appears to be incapable at times of resolving differences within the staff and the resultant inaction makes for delay. The recent confirmed appointment of a career employee as a Commissioner may provide some remedy for this situation. But it points up the absolute necessity for having qualified individuals as members of the Commission.

Rapidity of decision in many matters is more important in the Securities and Exchange Commission than in most of the other regulatory agencies. The failure to get a decision or delay in making a decision is in itself defeat in many cases. Delegation thus becomes essential. Too little of this characterizes the work of the Commission and, when it does exist, the line of delegation is not clear. Decisions, important decisions, are made by subordinates at fairly low levels and, because of time pressures of such importance to the business of financing, their decisions have to be accepted. On the other hand, in such simple matters as the acceleration of the effective date of registration statements decision is not delegated and unnecessary time is consumed by the Commission in dealing with a problem that in nine out of ten cases is simple of solution.

The Securities and Exchange Commission has an opinion writing section whose quality is high, if not the highest among the agencies. Nevertheless, it should be abolished and individual Commissioners held individually responsible for the enunciation of the grounds upon which conclusions of the

Commission are stated to rest. If the numerous speeches and articles of the various Commissioners are a test of their capacity for articulation, this should not be an impossible task.

The extension of the Commission's power of forcing appropriate disclosures with respect to securities in the over-the-counter market — an extension long urged by the Commission — is a matter for legislative action. As an ideal it has basic merit, particularly with respect to categories of securities, such as bank and insurance stocks, which have traditionally refrained from listing on the stock exchanges. As a practical matter, certain restraining lines have to be drawn, perhaps tighter than those presently suggested by the Commission.

From the standpoint of the formal Presidential action needed with respect to the Securities and Exchange Commission, the only thing required is further strengthening the powers granted to the Chairman in 1950 to the full extent heretofore suggested for the Interstate Commerce Commission and the implementation of its powers to delegate adjudicatory matters to hearing examiners and employees.

4. The Federal Trade Commission

The problems of the Federal Trade Commission, apart from its overlapping jurisdiction with the Antitrust Division of the Department of Justice and the Food and Drug Administration, are purely internal. Here, as in the case of the Interstate Commerce Commission, the Civil Aeronautics Board and the Securities and Exchange Commission, the powers of the Chairman should be increased and the Commission's authority to delegate decision-making implemented by Presidential action under the Reorganization Act.

In 1954, a reorganization of the Commission, known as the Howrey reorganization, took place following the recommendations of the management consultants, Robert Heller and Associates. A major aspect of this reorganization resulted in a fractionalization of the handling of cases before the Commission and has proved to be a failure. This is not only the opinion of practitioners but of members of the staff of the Federal Trade Commission. In 1956, Subcommittee No. 1 on Regulatory Agencies and Commissions of the Select Committee on Small Business of the House of Representatives commented on this reorganization (at page 28) in the following terms:

"New and more paperwork was provided for, following the reorganization which was recommended by Heller & Associates . . .

"Not only was the cost of operation of the FTC increased under this new reorganization by virtue of the increased paperwork as has been indicated, but the cost of operation of the FTC was also increased by virtue of the reorganization providing for new positions of high salaried people. Some examples of that are provided in the testimony before the subcommittee."

Not only were separate Bureaus of Investigation and Litigation set up but a system of "project attorneys" was introduced. The consequence of this is revealed by the following excerpt from a report on the operation of the Commission:

"For example, when the investigator submits the completed files, along with his recommendations, the case is reviewed by the Branch Manager and his assistant, by the project attorney, the Chief Project Attorney, by the Director of the Bureau of Investigation and his two assistants, by the trial attorney and by his superiors, the legal adviser, the Assistant Director, the

Associate Director and the Director of the Bureau of Litigation before it is ever forwarded to the Commission for action.

"In the entire procedure the attached Status Report on cases shows that of all these reviewers, the project attorney takes the most time. Over 40 percent of the project attorney's cases are over one year old. Only 20 percent of the cases in field offices, where the actual investigation is conducted, are that old."

"If Litigation and Investigation were consolidated and the project attorneys were eliminated, the reviewing process would be cut down to this: Investigator — Field Office Manager — Trial Attorney — Division Chief — Commission.

"At the same time, the project attorneys could be reassigned to the investigative or trial staffs. This would add thirty experienced attorneys to those staffs without any increase in payroll expense."

The trouble, however, lies even deeper than this. Because of the unfortunate early history of the Federal Trade Commission in the 1920's in which the courts bore down upon the loose procedures of the Commission, extensive records were made in false and deceptive practice cases before the Commission. This procedure has continued to this day with the consequence that protracted records and consequent delay characterizes the conduct of cases of this nature. If the advertiser of a drug states that "four out of five doctors" recommend it, to prove the falsity of such an allegation much massing of evidence ensues. This practice coupled with the fact that the Commission has no power to issue interlocutory cease and desist orders on the basis of a *prima face* case, significantly emasculates the Commission's power to deal with the spate of deceptive advertising that floods our newspapers, our periodicals and our air waves. Whereas in the securities field puffing is kept to a minimum, caveat emptor is rampant in the sale of other products, even those bearing directly upon the public's health. It is not suggested that rules governing the sale of securities should be applicable to the sale of other products, but, if we are interested in minimizing false and deceptive advertising, some sanctions more effective than those presently possessed by the Federal Trade Commission must be fashioned. The interlocutory cease and desist order appealable to a court would be a first step. Absent such a remedy, years can elapse before any action is taken and then the only penalty is an order to cease and desist.

Other areas of the Commission's jurisdiction raise more complex issues both of facts and of law. Issues arising out of the concepts of monopoly and the stifling of competition are never simple. But they are not so immediate in their impact on the public as false and deceptive advertising. Also, the Robinson-Patman Act is an extremely poorly drafted statute. The scope of its operation has been muddled rather than clarified by court decisions. Nor has the Federal Trade Commission been able to fabricate clear standards out of its mélange of generalities, qualified by proviso upon proviso. Remedial devices in this field can only be had from the Congress, which must make up its mind as to what this legislation is really intended to accomplish. Some better analyses of these problems could, however, be made by the Federal Trade Commission. The vigorous and imaginative leadership currently enjoyed by the Division of Trade Practice Conferences should be continued. This is a valuable supplement to the formal litigation activity of the Commission. The industry-wide consultation program can cure in a few weeks competitive ills that would require several years of formal litigation to cure.

A basic problem of the Federal Trade Commission relates to its overlapping jurisdiction in the antitrust field with the Department of Justice, and in the food and drug field with the Food and Drug Administration. Over the years, it is beyond question that the Antitrust Division of the Department of Justice has been more effective than the Federal Trade Commission. The grant of statutory authority to the Department of Justice is broader, although there are a few areas where it cannot reach practices that the Federal Trade Commission can handle. The sanctions that the Antitrust Division can invoke are far more powerful than those possessed by the Federal Trade Commission with the result that consent decrees can be better and more easily achieved by the Department of Justice.

In the food and drug field the jurisdictional areas of the Federal Trade Commission and the Food and Drug Administration are again not identical, but they do overlap. The sanctions available to each agency are also different, with a measure of greater power residing in the Food and Drug Administration.

The overlap in both these areas calls for correction. A sensible arrangement would be to transfer the antitrust activities of the Federal Trade Commission (not including its Robinson-Patman Act jurisdiction) to the Department of Justice, and to the Federal Trade Commission the duties of the Food and Drug Administration now in the Department of Health, Education and Welfare, provided, of course, that each transferee can demonstrate its capacity to conduct a vigorous program in the discharge of these new responsibilities.

An overlap is also alleged to exist between the Federal Trade Commission and the Federal Communications Commission in the field of false and deceptive advertising over the radio waves. This, however, is unimportant. The Federal Trade Commission has the responsibility to deal with false and deceptive advertising whatever the means of communication employed. Whether as a consequence of indulging in such practices the status of a Federal Communications Commission licensee should be altered, is an appropriate consideration for the Federal Communications Commission.

An overlap also exists between the Federal Trade Commission and the Department of Agriculture with regard to unfair trade practices of persons in the meat packing industry. There is no reason why full jurisdiction over the meat packing industry in that respect should not be returned to the Federal Trade Commission.

One prime reason for close contact between the Executive and the Federal Trade Commission through its Chairman is the fact that the Federal Trade Commission simply cannot cover all the areas of trade in which unfair practices are brought to its attention. It must concentrate on specific fields such as cigarettes, toys, or textiles. This involves an issue of policy of which the Executive should not only be aware but which should be keyed to whatever overall program is then the Administration's prime concern. The responsibility for concentration on a particular area should be the responsibility of the Executive and not the Federal Trade Commission.

5. The Federal Communications Commission

The Federal Communications Commission presents a some-what extraordinary spectacle. Despite considerable technical excellence on the part of its staff, the Commission has drifted, vacillated and stalled in almost every major area. It seems incapable of policy planning, of disposing within a reasonable period of time the business before it, of fashioning procedures that are effective to deal with its problems. The available evidence indicates that it, more than any other agency, has been susceptible to *ex parte* presentations, and that it has been subservient, far too subservient, to the subcommittees on communications of the Congress and their members. A strong suspicion also exists that far too great an influence is exercised over the Commission by the networks.

The quality of its top personnel is, of course, primarily responsible for these defects. The members of the Commission do not appear to be overworked in the sense that the Commission's docket is bulging with cases calling for disposition. Nevertheless disposition lags. Only 32 cases, all dealing with broadcasting licenses, were decided by the Commission during fiscal 1959, other than cases dismissed or in which the examiner's report became final. Commission action following the examiner's report in 9 of these cases took from 6 to 12 months and in 10 cases from one year to two years. In broadcast license cases no criteria for decision have evolved. True, criteria of various different kinds are articulated but they are patently not the grounds motivating decision. No firm decisional policy has evolved from these case-by-case dispositions. Instead the anonymous opinion writers for the Commission pick from a collection of standards those that will support whatever decision the Commission chooses to make.

Observers of the procedures employed by the Commission agree that the issues litigated are unreal and a mass of useless evidence, expensive to prepare, is required to be adduced. The uselessness of much of this evidence derives from several causes.

The first is that programming proposed by applicants is of high-sounding moral and ethical content in order to establish that their operation of a radio and television station would be in the "public interest". The actual programming bears no reasonable similitude to the programming proposed. The Commission knows this but ignores these differentiations at the time when renewal of licenses of the station is before them. Nevertheless, it continues with its Alice-in-Wonderland procedures. Also because of the varying standards that the Commission employs, a vast amount of unrealistic testimony is adduced to support each of these standards, incumbering the record with useless data.

On major policy matters, the Commission seems incapable of reaching conclusions. The UHF debacle has been plainly apparent for some 5 to 6 years. Nothing of any substantial consequence has yet been accomplished by the Commission to relieve the situation, although they are now purporting to make available additional VHF channels in one and two V-channel markets.

The procedures employed by the Commission in adjudicatory matters as well as in purely exploratory matters seem primarily at fault for these deficiencies. Leadership in the effort to solve problems seems too frequently to be left to commercial interests rather than taken by the Commission itself. No patent solution for this situation exists other than the incubation of vigor and courage in the Commission by giving it strong and competent leadership, and thereby evolving sensible procedures for the disposition of its business.

6. The Federal Power Commission

The Federal Power Commission without question represents the outstanding example in the federal government of the breakdown of the administrative process. The complexity of its problems is no answer to its more than patent failures. These failures relate primarily to the natural gas field, in the Commission's handling of its responsibilities with respect to the transmission and the production of natural gas. Enough has already been said about the delays in this field, so terribly costly to the public and so productive of unemployment in other basic industries.

These defects stem from attitudes, plainly evident on the record, of the unwillingness of the Commission to assume its responsibilities under the Natural Gas Act and its attitude, substantially contemptuous, of refusing in substance to obey the mandates of the Supreme Court of the United States and other federal courts.

The Commission has exhibited no inclination to use powers that it possesses to get abreast of its docket. Thousands of rate cases dealing with independent gas producers clutter its docket. Of this mass of cases Senator Paul H. Douglas of Illinois has pointed out that an exemption of producers of natural gas in interstate commerce for resale of less than 2 billion cubic feet per year would take 4,191 producers, whose total production of natural gas was only 9.26% of the total volume of gas purchased by interstate pipeline companies in 1953, out of the jurisdiction of the Commission. The portion of the total production accounted for by these small producers may have varied slightly since then but still remain insufficient to require then to be subjected to regulation in order to provide adequate protection to natural gas consumers against monopoly prices. Nevertheless, no effort has been made by the Commission to clear its docket of these inconsequential cases in order to come to grips with the relatively few remaining producers who do matter.

The recent action of the Commission on September 28, 1960 in promulgating area rates, whether ultimately legal or not, has come far too late to protect the consumer. The area prices there set forth substantially reject the rate base approach and the fixed area prices come close to approximately current maximum prices, which have more than doubled in the past five years. The Commission's past inaction and past disregard of the consumer interest has led the states to seek to force it to discharge its responsibilities. It is somewhat of a phenomenon in our national life for the state utility commissions to be ranged against a federal commission in an effort to protect consumers against monopolistic and excessive rates. That, however, is today's picture of federal regulations of the natural gas industry.

The transmission side of that industry presents the same picture. Delay after delay in certifications and the prescription of rates has cost the public millions of dollars.

An example of the inability of the Commission to control the. disposition of its business is afforded by the following.

A substantial number of certificate filings made by independent producers and pipelines request nothing more than the authority to make increased or additional sales of natural gas to existing customers or to customers within the same areas. These applications do not pose complex problems, but the paperwork and the dozens of steps taken while processing those applications contribute materially to the backlog which presently confronts the Commission. Not only do these relatively minor cases stack up, but also their presence delays Commission action on the other vital matters before it.

At the specific request of the Commission, the Congress amended the Natural Gas Act in order to provide a simplified procedure to cope with problems in this category. In 1942, in response to the Commission's urgent pleas. Congress enacted Section 7(f) of the Natural Gas Act which provided, in the plainest terms, that the Commission should determine "the service area" for a regulated company, and "Within such service area as determined by the Commission a natural-gas company may enlarge or extend its facilities for the purpose of supplying increased market demands in such service area without further authorization."

Under the procedure presented by Section 7(f), the Commission could readily eliminate thousands of unnecessary requests for authorizations. For example, even though an independent producer holds a certificate to sell gas to a pipeline from certain leases, the subsequent acquisition of additional leases requires the independent producer to obtain further authorization in order to increase its sales to the same pipeline. There is not a single instance in which this authority has ultimately been denied. Nevertheless, the Commission has needlessly required the filing of separate applications.

Similarly, the Commission requires the complete gamut of pleadings and processing in order to enable an established producer to sell gas from a new well to an established pipeline at a price completely in line with prices theretofore certificated.

An identical problem is posed to a pipeline which wishes to meet the increased requirement of a distributor, even though no change in rate is involved.

It was to do away with these problems that Section 7(f) was enacted. Nevertheless, during the 18 years that provision has been in the statute, the Commission has not utilized it on a single occasion.

In early 1942, applications were filed by five pipelines for service area determinations. Those applications have not been acted upon to this date. Of course, the same is true of every subsequent application under Section 7(f).

In 1944, the Commission attempted to justify its inaction on grounds that the wartime conditions required all available manpower for other purposes. However, the Commission added: "This work, on the determination of service areas should be pressed forward as vigorously as possible, as soon as the exigencies of war make it practicable for the Commission and the companies to conduct the necessary investigations and hearings."

Despite this and subsequent pious expressions, the Commission has literally done nothing to reduce the delays which have constantly increased. Instead, when Congress requested action the Commission merely addressed a letter on May 8, 1946 to all natural gas companies requesting their views regarding administration of the service area provision of the act. The Commission simply ignored the replies.

In January 1947, the Commission's staff prepared and submitted an extensive report to the Commission strongly recommending implementation of Section 7(f), and recommended the preliminary action be taken forthwith "to effectuate the intent of Congress expressed in Section 7(f)."

If the Commission has any legitimate reason for its 18 years of failure to implement Section 7(f), it has not given any expression thereto. Moreover, any possible criticism of the service area procedure provided by Congress at the Commission's request could readily be handled by the attachment of suitable conditions to service area determinations.

Other instances of ineffective administration are legion. Indeed, the dissatisfaction with the work of the Commission has gone so far that there is a large measure of agreement on separating from the Commission its entire jurisdiction over natural gas and creating a new commission to handle these problems exclusively.

It is probably unnecessary to go this far. However, certain amendments to the Natural Gas Act are essential. The Commission might well be increased to seven members so as to permit it to sit in two panels of three, with final decision in each panel, so as to help it clear up its enormous back log. But primarily leadership and power must be given to its Chairman and qualified and dedicated members with the consumer interest at heart must be called into service to correct what has developed into the most dismal failure in our time of the administrative process.

7. The National Labor Relations Board

When the National Labor Relations Act (Wagner Act) was enacted in 1935, its administration was vested in a National Labor Relations Board made up of three members. The Board appointed its own General Counsel, and the appointment and direction of the staff, both in Washington and in Regional offices, were vested in the Board. The Board handled all aspects of both unfair labor practices and questions of representation. Thus, the same agency determined what cases to prosecute, conduct the prosecution, and rendered the decision. This pattern of organization was the same as that of other, older administrative agencies like the Interstate Commerce Commission and the Federal Trade Commission. In practice, the prosecuting and adjudicating functions were separated by internal divisions in the staff in a manner fully consistent with the requirements of the Administrative Procedure Act, which was enacted in 1946. Indeed, only marginal changes in the Board's procedures had been required by the Administrative Procedure Act, the Board having administratively accomplished the appropriate separation of the prosecution and adjudicatory functions some years before the enactment of the Administrative Procedure Act.

In 1947, the Labor Management Relations Act (Taft-Hartley Act) was enacted. This Act, amending the Wagner Act, made a further separation between the prosecution and adjudicatory functions of the Board. It created the office of the General Counsel, to be filled by the President for a term of four years with the advice and consent of the Senate. The General Counsel was given the power to issue or withhold complaints and the entire legal staff, except legal assistants, appointed to assist Board Members prepare their decisions, was placed under his supervision. He also has general supervision of the Regional offices. The Board, expanded to five members, was continued as an administrative agency with powers to adjudicate upon complaints of unfair labor practices and with responsibility for handling all aspects of questions of representations, including the actual conduct of elections.

Since 1947 there have been no further statutory changes affecting the basic administrative pattern of the National Labor Relations Act.

There are, of course, various explanations as to why the administrative structure was changed in the foregoing manner in the Taft-Hartley Act. An Advisory Panel on Labor Management Relations Law to the Senate Committee on Labor and Public Welfare On The Organization And Procedures Of The National Labor Relations Board, established pursuant to a 1959 Senate Resolution, has stated with respect to the reasons for the change as follows in its January 1960 Report:

"In practice the prosecuting and adjudicating functions were separated by internal divisions in the staff. The functions merged only in the small percentages of cases in which the Board members themselves decided whether a complaint should issue, but regardless of whether this was intrinsically fair the emotional character of labor-management discussions, the controversies attendant upon the growth of strong unions and the spread of collective bargaining, and the suspicion of administrative bias, all lent color to the criticism that one body was acting as prosecutor, judge, and jury."

Others tend to the view that the forces which led to the enactment of the substantive provisions of the Taft-Hartley Act desired that a dominant voice in its administration should be given to a General Counsel subject to fresh confirmation by the Senate rather than to a Board which had been administering the statute prior to those amendments which were widely considered to be less than favorable to organized labor.

In any event, "the difficulty of administering one statute through two heads", to use the phrase of the Senate Committee's Advisory Panel, soon became apparent. In its January 1960 Report the Advisory Panel listed five "troublesome problems" which had engendered "controversies sufficiently bitter to erupt into public view":

(1) There were differences between the General Counsel and the Board concerning the exercise or declination of jurisdiction in unfair labor practices, the General Counsel taking the view that he alone had power to say when jurisdiction should be assumed, and the Board asserting the same power.

(2) There were disputes concerning the enforcement National Labor Relations Board orders, both responsibility for determining whether there was sufficient compliance with the Board's order, and in those cases where the General Counsel demurred at defending orders issued by the Board over his objection or upon a rationale which he regarded as unsound.

(3) There were differences which affected the interrelationship between questions of representation and unfair labor practice cases.

(4) There was "argument and dissension" concerning the appointment and control of staff in Regional offices.

(5) There were differences in connection with the General Counsel's refusal to issue complaints. "Although the Board might adopt one rule of law or policy, the General Counsel could easily thwart the Board's decisions by declining to issue a complaint based upon the Board's philosophy."

Summing up, the Advisory Panel concluded that "there is little doubt that the controversies between the General Counsel and the Board have hampered the enforcement of the National

Labor Board Act." These differences "are certain to continue so long as the present arrangement persists with the degree of intensity varying according to the personalities of individual officials." Accordingly, the Advisory Panel, which was composed of the most prominent authorities in the labor law field in the country, unanimously recommended "abandonment of the present hybrid compromise."

As the Senate Committee's Advisory Panel observed, revision of the present "two-headed" system may take either of two forms: The first, which was recommended by President Truman in a plan of reorganization defeated in the Congress in 1950, is to restore the pattern of organization of administrative agencies such as the Federal Trade Commission, relying upon the Administrative Procedure Act to guarantee sufficient separation between the prosecuting and adjudicating functions. In fact, this would mean a return to the administrative pattern before the Taft-Hartley Act, since the Labor Board had functioned in compliance with the Administrative Procedure Act before 1947. Alternatively, those functions now performed by the Board other than the adjudication of unfair labor practice cases, could be transferred to the General Counsel and his title changed to that of "Administrator". This would mean that he would secure complete control over all personnel, other than the Board and its legal assistants, and would acquire jurisdiction over representation cases in addition to retaining the General Counsel's present complete control over the issuance of complaints in unfair labor practice cases. This second solution represents the view of the Advisory Panel.

In its report, the Advisory Panel considered the advantages and disadvantages of each of these alternative solutions before deciding to recommend the second. It admitted frankly that a single administrative agency has the advantage of having "central direction of the manifold lines of activity which are required to implement a broad legislative policy," pointing out that such implementation involves not merely the adjudication of cases but also "the informal adjustment of charges, the selection and timing of cases or prosecution, decisions concerning the relative emphasis to be placed upon different aspects of the statute, the balance to be achieved between negotiated settlements and rigorous prosecution, and the presentation of cases in the courts." It emphasized that the lack of centralized direction of all phases of investigation, prosecution, adjudication and appellate litigation "would seriously hamper the development of programs under new social or economic legislation which are expressed in terms sufficiently general to leave scope for administrative discretion and the evolution of new legal concepts."

Despite these powerful arguments, the Panel nevertheless cited developments which in its view have reduced the occasion for unified control in the administration of the National Labor Board Act. The first such development cited by the panel was that since "most of the basic policies and legal concepts have now been established", administration now requires "emphasis on the enforcement of existing rules rather than the creation of new programs or principles" But in the very month (January 1960) in which the Advisory Panel talked about the crystallization of rules and indicated that what was necessary was emphasis on the enforcement of them, the General Counsel of the National Labor Relations Board stated, in a speech at the University of Minnesota, that "* * * on the substantive side of the law, we are today indeed in a period of transition, readjustment, and adaptation." And earlier, in November 1959 in addresses at San Francisco and in New York, he discussed in detail "the puzzling provisos" in the 1959 changes in the National Labor Act, relating to the barring of organizational picketing, secondary boycotts, the resolution of the Federal-State jurisdictional problem, the special provision relating to construction contracts, and other difficult areas of interpretation and administration caused by the 1959 substantive amendments to the Labor law. Nor were the 1959 Amendments the only area of uncertainties and creative administration As the General Counsel stated in his San Francisco speech.

". . . the General Counsel must, by the very nature of his position, make the initial interpretations of the law . . . Although most cases — and here I am speaking of those arising under the old law — are governed by established legal precedents, these are always a small but significant number of cases which present novel or difficult questions of law or policy. *These are the cases which are significant in the administration of the Act, and which give it full content and meaning.* After twelve years the meaning of the 1947 amendments in critical areas is still being litigated. . ."

The Advisory Panel also advanced what may have been a persuasive reason for its failure to support the first alternative solution to the present problem. It stated that "any return to the original set-up would revive old fears, justified or unjustified, of a one-sided tribunal serving as both prosecutor and judge."

The Advisory Panel's conclusions on this major issue follow generally the lines of the survey of the NLRB made by McKinsey and Company, Inc., Managerial Consultants, at the request of the Bureau of the Budget. Neither the conclusions of the Advisory Panel or the managerial consultants are too persuasive. Friction between the General Counsel and the Board, so continuingly serious, is not likely to be significantly reduced.

Their disparate positions are such that rivalry between them is inevitable. Nor can a separation be made between them with reference to the handling of unfair labor practice cases and representation cases since too frequently one controversy will involve both issues. A return to the earlier system, a conclusion reached in an excellent study by the Bureau of the Budget itself in 1958, seems preferable to the Advisory Panel's solution, although the latter would bring about improvements over what presently exists.

Inordinate delay and docket congestions of the type that characterizes the other major regulatory agencies is not the pattern of the business before the National Labor Relations Board. Figures covering fiscal year 1958 disclose that of the unfair labor practice cases filed, 88% are disposed of in the field in an average of 51 days by withdrawal, dismissal or settlement. Of the remaining 12%, in which formal complaints are issued, only 5.6% call for formal Board action. The average time for disposition from initiation of the complaint to final disposition, however, is too long being somewhat under 500 days. The record in representation cases is better. Although notices of hearing are issued in 46% of these cases, and 23% go to the Board after hearing, 18% of these are disposed of on the average by the short form proceeding within 80 days from the issuance of the notice of hearing and the balance of long form proceedings average some 120 days for final disposition.

Here again giving more effective finality to the examiner's finding is the answer. A suggestion to this effect is now pending before the Board in the form of certain recommended rules of practice drafted by a committee headed by Board Member Jenkins. But more finality can be achieved by a Presidential reorganization plan than by these proposals.

8. Other Regulatory Agencies

A particularistic analysis of other regulatory agencies is not included herein. Their problems are not generally like those of the agencies discussed above. The Federal Maritime Board, for example, raises different organizational problems, due to the executive responsibilities it possesses and the existence of a Maritime Administrator responsible to the Secretary of Commerce. But in its quasi-judicial aspects it suffers from a lack of settled, public procedures and standards of decision thus resulting in the exercise frequently of arbitrary powers by the staff. it places too much emphasis on bureaucratic details to the disregard of matters of large public importance. A fog of secrecy also surrounds many actions of the Board and no articulate standards seem to have developed with respect to *ex parte* presentations. Each agency, however, requires separate consideration and individual remedial action.

9. Action Immediately Desirable

These steps should now be taken:

(1) Reorganization plans should be prepared covering the agencies named above, strengthening the position of the Chairmen, having them designated in all instances by the President and holding the office of Chairman at the pleasure of the President. These plans should also include provisions permitting delegation of the decision making powers to subordinate officials, such as hearing examiners or employee boards, subject only to a limited administrative review by the agency itself. No effort should be made to affect the existing scope of judicial review.

(2) Budgetary needs should be carefully surveyed so that the work of the agencies should not be hampered by a false sense of economy.

(3) Further reorganization plans of a more extensive nature should be prepared dealing with the individual necessities of the various agencies. Those agencies in the worst situation such as the Federal Power Commission, the Federal Communications Commission, the Interstate Commerce Commission and the Civil Aeronautics Board, should be given preference. The responsibility for the preparation of these plans should be centered in the Office of the President. Enough formal studies and material now exists to enable the fashioning of these plans.

B. Personnel

The prime key to the improvement of the administrative process is the selection of qualified personnel. Good men can make poor laws workable; poor men will wreak havoc with good laws.

As long as the selection of men for key administrative costs is based upon political reward rather than competency, little else that is done will really matter. Thus, the real issues are two: (1) are these posts sufficiently attractive to draw good men, and (2) how can these men be found?

Good men are primarily attracted by the challenge inherent in a job. Salary is a secondary consideration, provided only that it is high enough to enable them to meet reasonable standards of living, comparable to their positions in the society. Our universities have known and, indeed, traded on these facts. Tenure is another consideration of more importance than salary, for with tenure goes independence and the opportunity for long-range planning.

Basic challenges have been missing in the last decade. Good men cannot be attracted to agencies if they see that the colleagues with whom they are called upon to work, the staffs that they must utilize, are not measurable by standards they believe to be appropriate. Such a condition implies a lack of concern or a lack of understanding of the regulatory process by the President, either or both of which are destructive of the very thing that could hold an appeal. The appeal of a job can also be destroyed if the President, through design or neglect, permits his prejudices in behalf of political associates or friends to dictate the deposition of individual items of business. No truly good man can submit to such interference. Finally, the job's relationship to the general program of the Administration must be clear and that clarity of relationship with the help of the President constantly maintained. These are the essential ingredients of the concept of challenge. They are also essential lures for the enlistment of talent.

Compensation is a consideration. Present salaries for top administrative personnel are in the neighborhood of $20,000 per year. This is a reasonable salary for the present level of the cost of living. Increasing it by $2500 or even $5000 would not appreciably affect the situation. But there are two things that could make these positions more attractive at a very reasonable cost. The first is the grant of a moderate entertainment allowance to the administrator. Like an ambassador he needs to maintain a certain prestige with the industry. He should be able to entertain rather than be required to suffer entertainment. At conferences, which he not infrequently is required to call, luncheon breaks should provide something better than service from a government cafeteria. The second matter is an adequate retirement allowance. For unexplained reasons the retirement allowance for executive employees is considerably less than the allowances available to legislators. As an alleged servant of the Congress, the independent Commissioner or his counterpart could be enfolded within the legislative scheme. This fringe benefit could well make a difference.

Chairmen, especially if their powers are enhanced, should be compensated on a better basis than their colleagues for they have more do to. The present difference rarely runs over $500 a year, a sum which is neither sufficient to be compensatory nor to make for prestige.

Tenure is of importance. A term of five or seven years is too short. If the appointee is a lawyer or in business, conflict of interest laws require him to sever all his past connections. To give up a practice patiently accumulated over the years is not easy. For it may well become necessary to spend years again in reestablishing it. To eliminate oneself from a place in the ascending ladder of a business organization raises similar problems. Moreover, longer tenures would mean opportunities for longer-scale planning, freedom from worry as to reappointment, and generally the concept of devotion to a career rather than that of a stepping stone to further political or professional advancement. Turnover would probably be reduced as is true of the members of the Federal Reserve Board whose tenures are fourteen years. Expertise would have a better chance to develop and the sense of security would inculcate the spirit of independence. Life tenure is, perhaps, too dangerous in these areas of dynamic activity but certainly a ten year term is not too much to suggest.

Given competent appointments to deal with real challenges which can be made to exist, the recruitment of a competent staff is not difficult. Great universities have never had their difficulties on this score and great administrative agencies could offer a similar challenge. Both should possess essentially the same opportunity of objectivity and the same urge to search for answers to pressing problems, with the balance, so far as the practically minded man is concerned, in favor of the latter. But the key to staff competence can only be found through the existence of inspiration and competency at the top level.

C. Ethical Conduct and Industry Orientation

Conflicts of interest appear not to be a serious problem in the regulatory agencies. As the Association of the Bar of the City of New York in its recent study of this general problem entitled "Conflict of Interest and the Federal Service", remarked: "The substantive regulations of many agencies show forth as relatively integrated, more modern [then the conflict of interest statutes], better drafted and, most important, as relevant expressions of public policy". The real problem centers about *ex parte* presentations.

The definition of what constitutes an undesirable *ex parte* presentation is not easy. As difficult is the definition of the circumstances under which such presentations can be appropriately made and those circumstances under which the making of substantially the same presentation is wrongful. The source of the presentation also bears on the factors as to whether it is wrongful or not. Again, there is the question of what sanctions should be employed against them and how to handle oral *ex parte* presentations as to which disputes will arise as to the fact, the manner and the nature of their utterance. Finally, there is the question of what sanctions should be employed to eradicate them.

Both houses of the Congress have recently been struggling with these problems and considerable refinement of the ways in which to define and deal with those that are wrongful has taken place. Further advances can be expected to be made as the next Congress is certain to return to the problem.

The issue here considered is whether action of any kind should be taken by the Executive with respect to this problem. Executive action would have the virtue of defining with some degree of particularity what conduct would constitute grounds for removal from the public service by the President or other persons empowered to remove public servants for cause. It would also presumably furnish a criterion for the action of professional associations, such as bar associations or boards of accountancy, in disciplining their members. It would not, however, reach the worst source of these presentations, namely the regulated industries themselves except insofar as their presentations might be made by persons in the organized professions. It would also not extend to Congressmen and Senators.

The only way in which these latter categories could be reached would be by the legislative creation of criminal sanctions. The objections to doing so lie in the difficulty of defining the crime and the difficulty of convicting guilty offenders. The latter is probably a difficulty but not a valid objection to action. Convictions under our anti-lobbying statutes are rare but they nevertheless have been useful in reducing the blatant lobbying practices that preceded their enactment.

Presidential action by way of executive order in this field appears desirable even though it is necessarily limited in its impact. But such an executive order should be couched in general terms. It should eschew any effort to enter into detail such as to seek to define when a proceeding becomes a proceeding on the record — a question now pending before the Civil Aeronautics Board and one which is likely to be carried to the courts. It should not seek to devise mechanisms for the manner in which allegedly oral *ex parte* presentations are to be made of record or circulated among interested parties who in many proceedings that number a hundred or more. Reputations can easily be irreparably damaged by well-intentioned but misguided or erroneous action.

The virtue of proscriptions generally worded is that they can and will be expounded in later proceedings and in the light of concrete situations. This is a field where circumstances will vary so markedly that we shall need to build slowly, brick by brick and case by case. But the President should initiate that process by laying the foundations for such a development through executive action.

Industry orientation of agency members is a common criticism, frequently expressed in terms that the regulatees have become the regulators. Of course, if this type of orientation characterizes an individual prior to his appointment, there is little that can be done about it. But the real problem relates to those who are originally oriented towards the public interest but who gradually and honestly begin to view that interest more in terms of the private interest. This is particularly likely to occur in agencies which in addition to their regulatory functions have promotional functions. It was manifested in the innate reaction of the Civil Aeronautics Board to the non-scheduled airlines and to the newer all-cargo air carriers. The Civil Aeronautics Board to date has not considered the provision of subsidy to these all-cargo air carriers. This is not a plea that it should urge the provision of such subsidy, but some rationalization for the grant of subsidy to local service carriers and its denial to the all-cargo air carriers should be made, since there is an obvious national interest in expanding the development of this branch of our transportation system. The Interstate Commerce Commission has frequently been characterized as railroad-minded, the Federal Communications Commission as dominated by the networks, while the actions of the Federal Power Commission speak for themselves.

This tendency toward industry orientation is subtle and difficult to deal with. It arises primarily from the fact that of necessity contacts with the industry are frequent and generally productive of intelligent ideas. Contacts with the public, however, are rare and generally unproductive of anything except complaint. For example, the public that our security legislation is designed to protect is the "investor", but the investor rarely appears and when he does he is too rarely an investor and too frequently a speculator who deserves exactly what happened to him.

Irrespective of the absence of social contacts and the acceptance of undue hospitality, it is the daily machine-gun-like impact on both agency and its staff of industry representation that makes for industry orientation on the part of many honest and capable agency members as well as agency staffs. A device, employed in some agencies, is some protection against this tendency. This is the device of the public counsel, the effectiveness of whose function is in almost direct relationship to his capacity to irritate the agency members. It should be encouraged, however, and the public counsel, in those cases where he has intervened, should be granted the right of seeking review from the decisions of trial examiners to the agency itself on terms accorded to the parties themselves, although a right to seek judicial review of decisions that have achieved finality should naturally be denied him since the public interest has presumably by that time coagulated in the agency's decision.

D. Administrative Procedure

Much work has been done in the field of improving administrative procedures since the passage of the Administrative Procedure Act of 1946. These improvements were preceded by intensive research and study. The chief contributors in this field have been organizations such as the Hoover Commission and various bar associations, scholars and individual practitioners. Much of the thinking by now has been fairly well crystallized and should soon be ready for formulation into legislation and administrative rules of practice and procedure. The difficulty presently is the absence of continuing effort and the lack of a point where such effort can be focalized so that action will ensue.

in 1953, the President sent out a call for a conference on the subject of administrative procedure which was attended by representatives of the various federal regulatory agencies, and distinguished members from the bench, the bar and the universities. A report was made by this conference in 1955 containing a series of important recommendations to the agencies as well as the Judicial Conference of the United States. With the close of the conference, there was no follow-up. However, one recommendation of the conference suggested that it, or something similar to it, be placed on a permanent basis and this recommendation was endorsed by the American and Federal Bar Associations as well as the Judicial Conference of the United States. On August 29, 1960, the President requested Judge Prettyman of the Court of Appeals for the District of Columbia Circuit to undertake the preliminary work of organizing such a conference. Judge Prettyman in turn appointed a committee of 14 members and has ready a preliminary draft of by-laws for such an organization.

This work should be encouraged and Judge Prettyman, whose knowledge of and devotion to the subject is well-known, should be requested to continue his efforts. Much can come from this effort, including not merely revisions in our administrative procedures but also the making of our regulatory agencies into a system just as the Judicial Conference of the United States has made a system of what were once isolated and individual federal courts. But for a conference of this type to be effective it is essential that a permanent secretariat be established, which can follow the work of various committees, break out issues and problems that require exploration and research, arrange for appropriate publications, and act as liaison agent between the conference, the Congress and the government generally.

The work and functions now lodged in the Office of Administrative Procedure in the Department of Justice should be transferred to this secretariat for the statistics can there be refined and reworked so as to make them significant to the operations of the conference. A second function now vested in the Civil Service Commission, that of the qualification and grading of hearing examiners, could also be transferred to this secretariat. The situation presently is admittedly a not too happy one. The Civil Service Commission is not fundamentally organized to handle this problem. The extremely important goals of maintaining the independence and integrity of the hearing examiners and of evolving a corps of highly qualified examiners can better be achieved through an arrangement of this character rather than leaving these problems to the Civil Service Commission.

Experiments in the flexibility of handling this corps and promoting a better use of examiners through an effort to make them at least partly fungible could be carried on by the secretariat and could make for uniformity and improvement in administrative procedures through the interchange of experience and knowledge. The secretariat could also be a central spot for the recruitment of lawyers for the government, particularly for the regulatory agencies.

The concept of an administrative Conference of the United States promises more to the improvement of administrative procedures and practices and to the systematization of the federal regulatory agencies than anything presently on the horizon. It could achieve all that the concept of the Office of Administrative Procedure envisaged by the Hoover Commission and endorsed by the American Bar Association hoped to accomplish, and can do so at a lesser cost and without the danger of treading on the toes of any of the agencies.

E. The Coordination of Agency Policy

Coordination of agency policy is meaningless in the absence of the internal development of policy by the individual agencies. The lack of such development in recent years has been commented upon and, in previous sections methods have been suggested as how that deficiency could be cured, namely the evolution of new procedures, the strengthening of planning divisions and the relief of agency members themselves from the multitudinous and frequently minor duties that they are required to perform.

In various areas, however, agency policies must be coordinated and welded into an integrated whole. Certain areas such as transportation, communication and energy are obvious areas where such coordination is essential. It has not infrequently been suggested that something akin to a Ministry or Department of Transportation with cabinet rank should be created. Many other countries have such departments and they are operated with considerable success. There are, however, striking differences between the situation in these countries and that which prevails in the United States. The area and scope of the problems differ decisively. No other nation possesses the vast network of surface transportation, both common carrier and private, that stretches over this country; nor does any nation possess the air route mileage or the vast fleet of planes maintained and operated by the people of the United States. But far more significant than this is the fact that the common carrier systems of these nations, with the exception of shipping, are generally owned and operated by their governments. We, on the other hand, have developed privately owned common carrier systems and have relied on the forces of competition to maintain these systems at their maximum efficiency. Our success in this approach has been generally recognized and, as a nation, we would be loathe to abandon it. The result is that in the transportation field our problems of controlling excessive competition, of restraining monopolistic practices, of promoting new forms of competition, do not raise controversies capable of internal settlement within the framework of a governmental bureaucracy. They present instead conflicts between various carriers' interests, between carriers and the public, and between carriers and the government. Beginning in 1887, we erected tribunals or administrative commissions to resolve these various conflicts and, because of the emergence decade after decade of new means of transportation, tribunals were created to deal with problems that at the time seemed capable of being handled most efficiently by specialists in particular fields. We are scarcely ready to reverse an approach that can over the years be regarded as having been successful simply because of the rising need for over-all planning and coordination.

Nevertheless, plans and blueprints for mechanisms such as a Department of Transportation have been in existence for years and new ones are being devised. None have as yet received substantial Congressional or Executive support. The blueprints, even the best of them, are unrealistic, beautiful in design but lacking in the appreciation of those earthy factors that are embedded in our regulatory transportation structure. Most of them entail the concept of some person in the nature of a czar sitting astride the whole transportation structure and exercising through subordinate bodies many of the functions now vested in the regulatory agencies. Others conceive of splitting away the adjudicatory functions but consolidating other functions in an executive department. It may be that we can eventually attain some such goal but the means of reaching it or an equally satisfactory goal must still be developed.

The history of the evolution of the War Production Board is of interest in this respect. That Board, although its machinery was not free from defects, successfully mobilized the greater part of our national productive plant for war purposes. We have had nothing in peace time that had as broad powers and as wide an area of concern as the War Production Board. It did not, however, spring Minerva-like from the brain of a Jove. Its evolution was painful and personal and institutional tragedies marked its coming into being. It had numerous antecedents such as the office of Production Management, the Supply Priorities and Allocation Board, and the National Defense Advisory Council, but eventually building upon the failures of these mechanisms, the War Production Board was brought into being and successfully survived the tremendous pressures generated by the demands of war. Similarly, the experiences of the Air Coordinating Committee laid the ground work for the Federal Aviation Act of 1958, a distinctly empiric piece of legislation.

If we would build towards the goal of coordinating our transportation system and its problems, we should do this carefully and on the basis of accumulating experience not merely as to problems but as to mechanisms to deal with these problems. A beginning along this line was made in 1953 by the creation in the Department of Commerce of an Undersecretary of Transportation. Although valuable work has been done in this office, that mechanism is probably not sufficient for the task. The reason is not necessarily the men who hold that office. It is the nature of the office itself. An office capable of doing such a task cannot be subordinate to the Secretary of Commerce, for its responsibilities are vaster and more important than all the other functions vested in the Department of Commerce. An arrangement of this nature makes achievement of these goals impossible. Such subordination destroys the very element of prestige necessary if leadership in this area is to evolve. It removes the fashioning of transportation policy one and even two steps from the President and, in so doing, permits the intrusion into that field of personages of lesser consequence weakening the sense of an authoritative approach to the problem as a whole.

The evolution of a national transportation policy must have a close and intimate relationship to the President. To do so by the creation of an executive department, however, means the imposition of presently undefined executive duties in the head of that department. These duties could probably be more defined at a later date in the light of experience and then vested without too much controversy in an appropriate governmental unit. Meanwhile, development of the coordinating function could be placed in the Executive Office of the President. It should not be vested in a White House assistant because such coordinating activity needs protection from trivia, from personality conflicts and even from polities, as well as the objectivity of approach that can be given the coordinating authority by vesting it in an office already constituted to perform staff and not personal functions for the President. The office would need no regulatory powers. It does need the constant personal support of the President and through him the President's Cabinet and the Bureau of the Budget. Given these, a coordination of policy can be effected by such an office among the various regulatory agencies, implemented where necessary by executive order. And, as experience demonstrates, coordination and consolidation of functions among them can be effected by the wise use of the President's power under the Reorganization Act.

A tentative program of what could be accomplished through such an office by way of immediate objectives and longer range objectives follows. A minimum of legislation is required for the immediate objectives. The longer range objectives may call for revision of policies hitherto established by Congress and fundamental legislative changes.

Among the immediate objectives are the following:

A. The achievement of a program for the amelioration of interurban public transportation, including the establishment of metropolitan transit commissions with federal aid in the form of matching guaranteed loans for the acquisition and improvement of facilities and equipment under sound engineering, operating, and financing plans.

B. Formulation of policies to coordinate Federal highway aid programs with approved metropolitan transit plans, so as to promote the economic soundness and efficiency of metropolitan public transportation systems as a whole, with emphasis on the avoidance of traffic congestion and the decline of public transportation.

C. Rationalization of government transport needs, including military transportation, so as not to compete with the commercial systems.

D. Evolution of Federal, State and local tax policies to assure that tax relief to railroads is compensated for in improved service.

E. Formulation of policies, through the establishment of joint service boards, to encourage through-routing and joint-service among and between all forms of freight transportation, with simplification of billing and freight charges.

F. Formulation of policies relating to approval of consolidations and unification of carriers, both within and between different modes of transportation, which give greater weight to reduction of transportation costs and improvement of service.

G. Formulation of policies with respect to the approval of abandonment of railroad routes or services, and the curtailment of service, to assure that the needs of the affected traffic are adequately served by other transportation.

H. Establishment of a coordinated statistical gathering, processing, and analytical service to provide reliable domestic transportation data for policy formulation and rate regulation. Such a service does not now exist.

I. Review and revision of the policies of the Army Corps of Engineers with respect to river and harbor maintenance and improvement to discourage the uneconomic expansion of outport facilities.

J. Re-examination of Merchant Marine subsidy policies to reduce uneconomic competition on over-expanded trade routes in foreign commerce.

Among the longer range objectives are the following:

A. Revision of Section 4 of Part I of the Interstate Commerce Act to modify or abolish the authority of the Commission to grant railroads relief against water carrier competition.

B. Modification of the statutory powers of the Interstate Commerce Commission and the Civil Aeronautics Board in the matter of granting certificates of convenience and necessity, to require as the basis for granting or withholding certificates and permits, greater reliance upon a statistical showing of operating costs, quality of service, and ability of efficient carriers to expand, rather than mere customer support, too often artificially inspired.

C. Steps to establish cost of service, as the principal factor for determining the reasonableness of transportation rates.

D. Formulation of a policy for regulating the entry of private carriers into the field of domestic surface transportation, and revision of the present statutory exemptions.

E. Formulation of a program of financial aid to distressed railroads to take the place of Chapter 19 of the Interstate Commerce Act (49 U. S. C. 1231) with revision to ensure that the borrower will have a sound capital structure, and that improvements in equipment and service will result from the financial aid.

F. A reconsideration of the field of user charges for federal facilities, particularly as regards air carriers, trucks and inland waterways.

G. Foreign carrier competition both by sea and by air and the evolution of policies as to the position that American carriers should rightly occupy in this field.

The equivalent of cabinet meetings at a sub-cabinet level of the more important agency chairmen would contribute to the development of a sense of cohesion among the agencies. The office in turn at stated periods would be called upon to report progress or the lack of it to the President and his Cabinet.

Similar approaches can be made by the creation of similar offices for the areas of communications and energy. In communications the lack of coordination in both the international and national field is apparent. Neither the State Department nor the Office of Civil and Defense Mobilization is capable of affording the necessary leadership. Their other activities are too varied to permit communication to reach the high level of concern that it must reach. Indeed, only this month a staff report prepared for the Senate Committee on Aeronautical and Space Services made as one of its prime recommendations: "The most careful and comprehensive study should be undertaken by the Executive Branch without delay to examine elements of public policy concerned with communications specifically as related 81 to (a) the identification of central Federal authority for communication policy . . ."

Time, tide, and space wait for no man and it may be later than one thinks.

It is unnecessary here to sketch out a program of coordinating activities in the communications and energy fields. Ample need for coordinated activities exists and the objectives are reasonably clear. Indeed, stagnation is apparent in many fields because of the lack of such coordination. In the energy field, however, emphasis should be placed upon the development of new sources of energy such as the hydrogenation of coal and oil-bearing rocks and also upon the wider employment of atomic energy. In the light of our dwindling water resources the need for energy to distill fresh water from the sea to make our arid areas fertile, is a commanding objective — a new frontier of untold significance to us and the world.

F. Relationship of the Agencies to the Executive and the Legislative

Some of the relationships of the agencies to the President have been sketched out in the preceding sections of this Report. The policy planning of those agencies engaged in the areas of transportation, communications, and energy, respectively, would be geared to the President as indicated through the offices to be established in the Executive Office. These offices concern the coordination of policy.

The development of detailed plans for the reorganization of the administrative agencies and continued oversight of these activities remains to be considered. Such oversight as is exercised by the Bureau of the Budget is at too low a level and extends substantially only to managerial functioning. The areas in which the agencies fail or hesitate to formulate policy presently tend to go unnoticed, as do those overlaps that have developed or are in formulation.

Congestion of dockets, time-consuming procedures, duplica-
tion of facilities and effort, and failures to delegate run-of-the-
mine problems all have to be watched. This function of the
President must be focused somewhere. The Bureau of the
Budget is not the appropriate place. A hostility inevitably
arises between the Bureau of the Budget and the agencies from
the very existence of the Bureau as the watch dog of potential
expenditures. What is needed is the development of an urge
for adequate reorganization on the part of the agencies and to
do so there must be engendered a desire to that end through
the existence of a cooperative atmosphere. The function of
exercising oversight should be in firm but friendly hands and
the office that exercises it a protagonist of the agencies before
the Bureau of the Budget, the President and the Congress. The
person charged with these responsibilities should not be a
mere Inspector-General but also a source of imaginative and
creative activity. Lodging that function in the Executive Office
of the President independently of the Bureau of the Budget
and transferring to that office the functions now exercised by
the Bureau of the Budget of managerial assistance is the
solution.

Presidential concern, with the work of the agencies, is important both from the standpoint of the President's duty to see
that the laws are faithfully executed and from the standpoint
of the morale of the agencies for they will then realize how
important their activities are to the national scene. To neglect
these agencies is to encourage the centrifugal tendencies
inherent in the "administrative branch" of the government and
to lessen their capacity to draw good men into their service.

Their relationship to the Congress would similarly be improved by the suggestions heretofore made. Congress will still
have to concern itself with innumerable details, for details are

the grist of the legislative mill. But in exercising its general functions of oversight, the function that President Wilson termed one of the most important of the duties of the Congress, the woods are too often obscured by the trees. This is inevitable if the general design of the activity of these agencies is obscured, for then their operations are viewed in a fragmentized fashion by the various different committees and sub-committees of the Congress. It is the design that is of prime importance to the Committees on Government Operations and that design will be far more clearly and effectively comprehended if the suggestions heretofore made are carried out.

One matter needs further comment. The fact that the Executive Office of the President will play a large part in the architectonics of particular administrative programs should not be utilized as a basis for the claim of executive immunity from Congressional scrutiny. The establishment of national goals to be effective must involve, as President Roosevelt so aptly observed, teamwork between the Executive and the Legislative. That teamwork should carry down to all levels. Weaknesses in planning or in the execution of plans are a matter of broad public concern and the Congress has its duty to discover and divulge these weaknesses, assess the blame for their occurrences, and assist in making such provisions as it can for their cure.

SUMMARY AND CONCLUSIONS

A number of suggestions with reference to improving the organization and procedures of certain of the regulatory agencies are contained in the above report. Many of these recommendations can be adopted, if deemed desirable, by action of the agencies, themselves; others can be incorporated in the plans for reorganization to be prepared as suggested below and are therefore not repeated in this summary.

But there are certain matters that need immediate attention, such as administrative delays and the lack of policy formulation both within an agency and among various agencies. An answer that can be made to the co-ordination of inter-agency activities is the consolidation of their various functions within a new Department. Such an answer may eventually be the right answer to many of the situations herein detailed. It was the answer made in 1953 by the creation in the Department of Health, Education and Welfare and the consolidation within it of functions formerly widely dispersed. But the beginnings of that project go back thirty years to a recommendation by President Harding in 1923. The present needs are too pressing to await the initiation of what would be a mammoth project of consolidation in the fields of transportation, communication, and energy and even a huge project in any one of them. The prime and immediate need in these fields is for developing and coordinating policy immediately at a high staff level. Operations for the moment can be left to the existing agencies, whose conduct should in the light of these recommendations show marked improvements. If experience later would dictate the desirability of the consolidation of certain operating functions, they will then have become sufficiently identified and understood to enable their intelligent consolidation in an appropriate departmental structure. To attempt such consolidation in the absence of the experience that would be derived from determined effort to evolve policy through coordination directly under the President, would be substantially to plan *in vacuo*. The creation of a mechanism for staff coordination can and should begin now. Its staff work as envisaged herein will carry within itself means for the implementation of its direc-

tives. With this thought in mind, the following recommendations are made:

1. Secure for the President from the Congress the right to
propose reorganization plans pursuant to powers heretofore
granted the President under the Reorganization Act of 1949,
subject to veto by a concurrent resolution of both Houses of
the Congress. The powers to propose plans should be available
for a minimum of two years but preferably for four years.

2. Propose a reorganization plan for the Interstate Commerce
Commission whereby its Chairman will be designated by the
President and serve as Chairman at his pleasure.

3. Propose a reorganization plan for the Federal Power
Commission making clear that the tenure of its Chairman is at
the pleasure of the President.

4. Propose reorganization plans for the Interstate Commerce
Commission, the Civil Aeronautics Board, the Federal Communications Commission, the Federal Power Commission, the
National Labor Relations Board, the Federal Trade Commission, and the Securities and Exchange Commission which will
make clear that the Chairman's authority extends to all
administrative matters within the agency, including responsibility for the preparation and review of its budget estimates,
the distribution of appropriated funds according to major
programs and purposes, and the appointment of all personnel,
except (i) those whose appointment is by statute vested in the
President, (ii) division heads whose appointment must be
confirmed by a majority of the agency members, (iii) special
assistants, not in excess of three, to each of the members,
which appointments shall be made by the respective members.

5. Propose reorganization plans for the same agencies providing for the delegation to panels of agency members, single agency members, hearing examiners or boards of employees for final determination all adjudicatory matters subject only to discretionary review by the agency *en banc* on petition by a party in interest.

6. Create within the Executive Office of the President with appropriate powers an office for the Coordination and Development of Transportation Policy to develop and implement a national transportation policy. This should be accomplished by a reorganization plan transferring to this Office all the responsibilities now vested in the Undersecretary of Commerce for Transportation.

7. Create within the Executive Office of the President with appropriate powers an Office for the Coordination and Development of Communications Policy and simultaneously by executive order transfer to this Office all powers relating to telecommunications now vested in the Office of Civil and Defense Mobilization.

8. Create within the Executive Office of the President with appropriate powers an Office for the Coordination and Development of Energy Policy with authority to propose to the President plans for the development of the energy resources of this nation.

9. Create within the Executive Office of the President with appropriate powers an Office for the Oversight of Regulatory Agencies which will assist the President in discharging his responsibility of assuring the efficient execution of those laws that these agencies administer.

10. Abolish the present President's Advisory Committee on Government Organization.

11. Abolish the positions of such Special Assistants to the President who have heretofore had as their major concern matters within the purview of the Offices to be created under recommendations 6, 7, 8 and 9.

12. The offices mentioned in recommendations 6, 7, 8 and 9 can be substituted for the Office for Emergency Management, which in its present form can be abolished.

13. Impose upon the Office for the Oversight of Regulatory Agencies the duty to prepare for the President detailed reorganization plans for the regulatory agencies with prime emphasis on the Federal Power Commission, the Interstate Commerce Commission, the Civil Aeronautics Board, and the Federal Communications Commission.

14. Issue an Executive Order dealing with the ethics of government employees and their duty to reject and refrain from receiving *ex parte* presentations in pending matters before them for adjudication on the record, which Order should specifically prohibit any such *ex parte* communication by any person in or part of the offices created under recommendations 6, 7, 8 and 9.

15. Promote the organization of the Administrative Conference of the United States and subject to the approval of its by-laws initially by executive order and subsequently by legislation provide for the creation of a Secretariat to the Conference, transferring to that Secretariat duties now performed by the Office of Administrative Procedure within the Department of Justice, which would thus be abolished and transferring from

the Civil Service Commission to the Secretariat duties now exercised by the Commission with respect to the qualifications and grading of hearing examiners.

16. Require the submission to the Congress and President of annual reports by the offices created pursuant to recommendations 6, 7, 8 and 9.

Respectfully submitted,

James M. Landis

ABOUT THE AUTHOR

James McCauley Landis (1899–1964) was a lawyer, law professor, government official, and legal advisor. More specifically, he was a professor of law and Dean at Harvard Law School and served in various government positions as part of the New Deal, as well as in the Truman Administration. He also served as Special Counsel to President John F. Kennedy.

In 1960, Landis drafted this Report to President-elect Kennedy, reexamining the federal regulatory commissions and administrative agencies' structures and powers. He recommended such reforms as strengthening the commissions' chairpersons and streamlining the agencies' procedures. The Kennedy Administration subsequently adopted many of the recommendations.

James M. Landis, circa 1938

qp

www.ingramcontent.com/pod-product-compliance
Lightning Source LLC
Chambersburg PA
CBHW031437270326
41930CB00007B/752